CATS & KITTENS

CATS & KITTENS

Joan Moore

REBO PUBLISHERS

Text: Joan Moore
Photographs: Marc Henri
Illustrations: Rod Ferring
Index: Caroline Eley
Layout: Consortium, England
Pre-press services: AdAm Studio, Prague The Czech Republic
Proofreading: Sarah Dunham

Acknowledgements: Grange Cat Homes, Hillier Garden Centre,
Woodhouse, UK (see the cat home on pages 36-37)

ISBN 13: 978-90-366-1557-0
ISBN 10: 90-366-1557-7

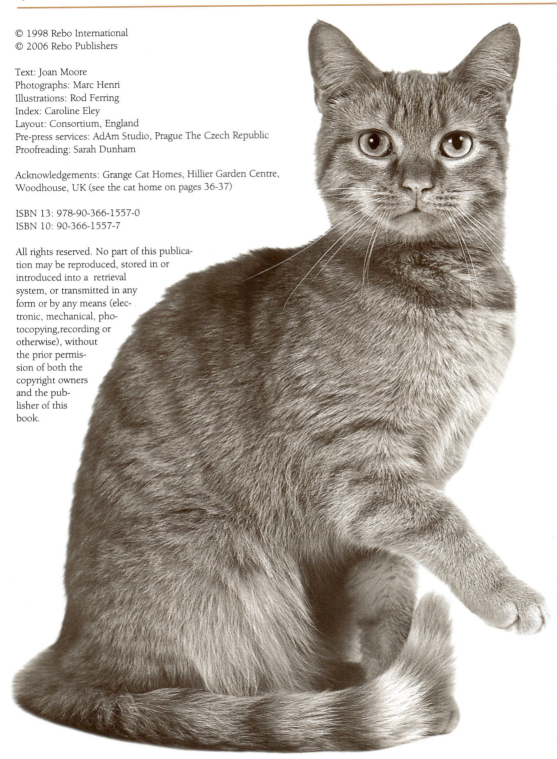

Contents

The Nature of Cats

By their very nature, cats make perfect companions. They are a part of our lives in a quiet, undemanding way. They are clean, companionable, aesthetically pleasing and readily catnap for approximately 16 hours out of every 24!
With their easy adaptability to most environments and lifestyles, either ensconced in a caring home or living out a feral existence, we admire the cat's independent spirit and natural-born instinct for survival. Not surprisingly, the domestic cat, in all its delightful forms, has gained a well-deserved place in our hearts to become, in many parts of the world, our most preferred companion animal.

Joys of ownership

Providing that your choice of feline friend is appropriate to your circumstances and environment, a truly rewarding lifelong relationship can develop. By understanding and respecting the underlying instincts and needs of your cat and given that these are met with your own, and those of your family, a happy compromise can be reached, making that relationship into something very special indeed.

Understanding each other

From the moment you say "welcome home" to your cat or kitten, it is kinder to keep to a regular regime in terms of meals and playtime – taking into account the times when you yourself wish to relax. House rules made early on in the proceedings suit kitty's "biological clock" and provide a comforting framework for its days – and nights! Understanding your feline friend's need for space – and that of your own – makes for a healthier and less frustrated relationship.

Meeting your children and other household pets can present an upsetting experience for the cat or kitten new to your home. Sensible handling, such as early, supervised introductions, are advised. Also, allowing for the cat's natural predatory instincts, birds and fish should be suitably secured at all times.

Never underestimate the intelligence of your cat. While scientists rarely acknowledge that cats possess that "sixth sense," it is part of their appeal for us that cats are extremely insightful and can very quickly sense our moods.

In harmony

Perhaps because of their intuitive qualities, cats make the ideal companion for our hours

of solitude, resting quietly by our side or on our lap, whiling away many happy, contented hours. Conversely, certain types of cat, generally the Oriental breeds, can be taken for walks on a harness and lead! This subject will be looked at in more detail later in the book, and it will be demonstrated how yet another dimension can add joy and fulfillment to the cat-human relationship!

Cats as therapy

It is a medically acknowledged fact that stroking cats can reduce the human heart-rate, lower blood pressure and generally enhance personal well-being and improve feelings of self-worth. Health workers and cat carers regularly take cats to rest homes and homes for the elderly in order to carry out this excellent work. Perhaps the aged and less mobile human patient can

recall a time when a cat was part of their daily life – and re-living happy memories is no bad thing, is it?

Quality time

We have all experienced those precious moments – relaxing in an easy chair, reading a favorite book with kitty on our lap, with his or her warm, purring body vibrating under our hand. The beneficial effect of this quality time is self-evident as we then go about our chores in a happier and more balanced frame of mind – undisputed evidence of and some very sound reasons why cats are so popular today!

Simply watch your cat in everyday mode: sleeping, stretching, grooming, soaking up the sunlight in a warm secluded spot or, perhaps, tending her kittens. The graceful movements and the restful repose touch our subconscious selves and make us feel so much better for it.

Cat characteristics

Each cat has its own unique personality and . . .
- its own method of communicating
- is discriminatory in its choice of humans
- will groom to hide its embarrassment
- enjoys brief periods of light sleep (catnaps)
- may stand on its back legs when it greets you
- is very inquisitive
- will open cupboard doors
- prefers scrunched-up paper to expensive toys
- generally sits on laps of people who do not like it
- adores sleeping in very small, dark places – and with humans!

Movement and Balance

Cats are one of the most graceful of all animals – every movement is an integrated poem of precision and beauty. The cat's body is also a super-efficient hunting machine. It can leap, climb, pounce and run swiftly with the utmost ease.

Using their claws and strong hind legs to climb trees, they can jump down from reasonable heights in comparative safety. It would not be true, however, to say that cats can leap down from unusually great heights without hurting themselves. They are as likely as any animal to sustain injury in these instances.

The hind legs

When a cat walks, its propulsion, or forward movements, are instigated by their powerful hind legs. Whether walking, trotting or running, the body is propelled forwards by the hind legs. The forelegs act as brakes and regulate the speed required. When trotting, the right front leg and the hind left leg move forwards together and vice versa. When running, the hind legs push forwards together.

Cats are surefooted and have an excellent sense of balance. They can run along narrow walls, fence tops and tree branches with apparent ease and hardly ever put a paw out of place.

However, were the cat to fall, its flexible backbone is made up of numerous bones held together by muscles which make the back very flexible and enable the cat to flip and twist on its descent. This way it falls curled up in a ball with back arched.

Resilience and flexibility

The consummate acrobat, the cat has up to 26 more vertebrae than the human, thus accounting for its superb flexibility. Shoulder-joint design enables the forelegs to turn in any direction, and unlike us humans, the cat lacks the conventional clavicle or collarbone, having only a vestigial one „floating" deep in the breast muscle. This enables the cat to squeeze through narrow spaces and also serves to lengthen its stride, if necessary.

Powerful leg muscles, especially the hindquarters, enable the cat to leap and jump with well-timed precision. These strong hindquarters also enable the cat's spectacular vertical jump. Here, the cat assesses the height in question and calculates how much propelling power from the hind legs is required.

Other useful attributes

Not only is the cat's skeletal make-up important in assisting its flexibility, balancing skills and other assets essential to its safety and survival, there are also other areas of the cat's body which play an integral part in the efficiency of its movements.

Whiskers The whiskers, or vibrissae, not only indicate moods but more importantly, in the survival stakes, act as antennae or feelers to help the cat judge widths through which its body passes. Whiskers can also be very expressive and their move-

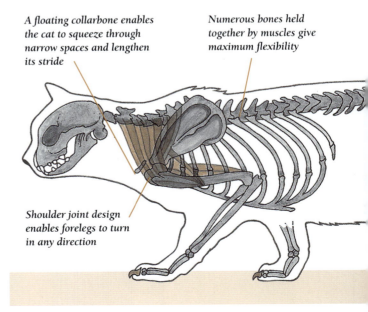

A floating collarbone enables the cat to squeeze through narrow spaces and lengthen its stride

Numerous bones held together by muscles give maximum flexibility

Shoulder joint design enables forelegs to turn in any direction

The "righting" reflex

• This "survival technique" is an instantaneous response and put into action when the cat falls from a height which is not comfortably accomplished by simply jumping down.
• The success of this exercise depends on the cat's keen eyesight, flexible backbone, muscle resilience and general suppleness.
• The "flip," as previously described, can be completed within approximately 60 cm (2 ft) of the cat's fall.
• Forelegs touch the ground first while the flexible shoulders absorb the impact. Hind legs follow and the back arches.
• The cat's joints and soft paw pads act as further shock absorbers.

The unsheathed claw

Each claw is attached to a toe bone. To unsheath the claw, leg muscles pull the tendons which then extend the toe and claw outwards.

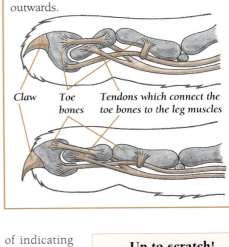

Claw   Toe   Tendons which connect the
          bones   toe bones to the leg muscles

Tail used to maintain cat's superb balance

Powerful leg muscles enable cats to leap and jump with precision

ments are a way of indicating when a cat is frightened, annoyed or simply inquisitive.

Paws Cats use their paws when feeding, washing, playing, climbing and hunting. The cat's paw is a very complex structure. The forepaw comprises five toe pads, five claws and two larger pads. The fifth claw, acting like a human thumb, is essential in climbing and for clutching and holding on to prey. The hind paw comprises four toe pads, four claws and one large paw pad.

The claws are curved, very sharp and with a few exceptions, such as in the Siamese cat, they are sheathed when not in use. The paw pad is also used to "scent mark" the cat's boundaries, for example on fences, trees and gate posts.

Up to scratch!

When you see your (enviably) supple cat with legs and claws outstretched and hindquarters reaching for the sky, he or she is exercising and s-t-r-e-t-c-h-ing those vertebrae, much as the human does when practising their aerobic exercises!

Tail A cat's tail may be long or short and in some cases, as in the Manx, absent altogether, but its importance should not be under-estimated. This useful item is essential to the cat. The tail is a flexible extension of the cat's spine and is used to maintain balance. It serves as a "rudder" while swimming and is indispensable in the expression of moods.

The Feline Senses

Sight

While it is said that the cat sees only in shades of grey with a minimal response to color, it is an extremely successful nocturnal hunter animal with eyes intricately designed to utilize any available light. Like other carnivores, including humans, its eyes are set forward, but it has a wider angle of vision than the human, allowing it to judge distances accurately and detect the slightest movement from potential prey. On night-time forays, their luminosity or shining mirror effect is caused by a reflective substance called the *tapetum lucidum*, which is located behind the retina. The pupil of the cat's eye opens and appears round in darkness to allow more light rays to enter. Conversely, in daylight, the pupils close to slits to exclude much of the light.

Touch

The cat's sense of touch is very perceptive – it receives sensory feedback when its guard hairs come into contact with an object. Whiskers, too, having sensitive nerve endings in the shaft base, offer a multitude of information when the cat comes into contact with objects. These can also pick up air movements and are indispensable when the cat is hunting. Whiskers can communicate moods and other messages to prey and other cats. A smaller group of whiskers can be seen on the underside of the forelegs. These have sensory usage while stalking and judging distances when jumping and leaping. Facial whiskers above the eyes and on the cheeks are touch-sensitive and warn of dangers to the exploring cat.

Hearing and balance

The cat is endowed with super-sensitive hearing – an essential faculty while hunting and exploring. With some 20 muscles working the pinna, or exterior of the ear, it acts as a swivelling "trumpet," homing in on the minutest sound such as the high-pitched squeak of a mouse or the faintest rustling movement.

The inner ear is the vestibular organ of balance, so this, too, assists the cat when climbing trees or performing other balancing feats on its nocturnal patrol. The flexible movements of the cat's ear also allows it to express a wide range of emotions and is used to communicate these feelings to ourselves and to other cats.

As in the human, the cat's hearing can deteriorate with age, when it loses the ability to hear the higher frequencies.

Eyes set forwards, to give a sense of depth and distance, and adaptable to changing light conditions – open pupils for night-time vision, narrowed pupils for bright light or daytime

Acute sense of hearing; special muscles enable the ears to rotate independently to detect prey or potential danger

Whiskers detect close prey movement, interpret widths through which the cat passes and express certain moods

Cat's taste and smell are linked because the nasal canal opens into the mouth; the Jacobson's organ is an extra taste/smell device situated in the roof of the mouth

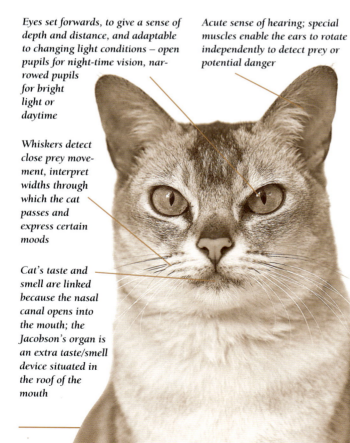

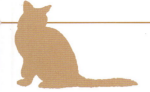

Smell and taste

Cats have an acute sense of smell, though it is not so acute as that of the dog. From kitten-hood, the cat's nose is used to detect its mother and her all-essential milk, its siblings and familiar surroundings. Later, the cat's sense of smell is used to detect potential danger, to identify friend from foe and to read "messages" left by the urine and feces of other animals. The surface of the cat's tongue is rough and the sides, tip and back of the tongue and part of the throat contain mounds of tissue called papillae. As well as being an aid to eating and grooming, these special sensory detectors assess temperature and taste. Most mammals can detect sweet, sour, salty and bitter tastes, but of these, the cat has little ability to detect sweet ones.

The Flehmen response

Another method of "smelling" is via the vomeronasal, or Jacobson's organ. This is situated within the hard palate which forms the roof of the mouth. When in use, the cat lifts its head and adopts a gaping, grimacing open-mouthed posture. The tongue may move in a lapping motion, aiding the scent to be wafted into the mouth. This "extra sense" prompts the Flehmen response described above.

Intelligence

We have seen that the cat is a finely tuned stalking, hunting

Pawnote:
Cats whose brains receive enhanced mental stimulation have larger brain bulk. But this does not indicate more brain cells, simply that there are more connections between existing cells.

and killing machine – its skeleton, muscles and keenly honed senses make it so. History and mythology indicate that the cat can be one of the most intelligent, and wily, of all animals. It can also be the most loyal of creatures; heart-rending tales of a mother cat's undying devotion to her young make typically poignant reading. So what really makes the cat the perceptive, super-efficient being that it is?

IQ tests

Scientific tests carried out to assess the intelligence of cats reveal that they do not generally respond to verbal praise, since this has no advantage to them in their natural role as a solo hunter, relying as they do on their own assessment of a situation and subsequent appropriate action. Their instinctive response to a food reward, however, is more positive. Similar tests with dogs have led to the presumption that dogs are more intelligent than cats. This is an unfair proposition since the nature of dogs is to please, while the cat often remains aloof and somewhat unresponsive to training and "verbal and stroking" incentive/reward techniques.

Instinctual and learned

The biological set-up of feline instincts and hormones which predetermines a cat's behavior patterns is genetically implanted and, therefore, present at birth. From its mother, the kitten progressively learns how to develop and utilize these instincts and skills. By the time we intervene in its upbringing, at approximately 12 weeks of age, the kitten is ready to absorb the second stage of its "education" – that of socializing with humans and accepting (to them) the unnatural restrictions and limits within the human household. Much of its future behavior depends upon the success of this stage.

The brain

The cat's brain receives all the information from the body's senses and hormone-producing glands. In turn, it interprets these signals and tells the body how to respond to this input via the nervous system.

The cat's brain comprises three sections: the forebrain, mid-brain and hindbrain and behaves like a biological computer. Besides being an immense repository of information, it contains billions of special neuron cells with some 10,000 connections to other cells. An important constituent is the pituitary gland, partly controlled by the hypothalamus – the neural control centre. It produces hormones which control body and fetal growth.

CHAPTER 1

Acquiring a Cat

Whether you are looking for a pedigree or a non-pedigree cat or kitten, it is essential that the feline you ultimately choose to share your life with is one that fits in with you, your family and your particular lifestyle. After giving each of these factors some careful consideration, you can then begin your search. Do remember that if you pine for a cute little kitten, it will quickly grow into an independent adult which could be with you for 12-15 years or more, so it is essential to make the right decision.

Since, naturally, your requirement is for a healthy, well-behaved feline friend, you will need to find a suitable source of obtaining the cat or kitten of your choice.

For the inexperienced cat owner, knowing just where to look, who to ask and how to choose a reliable source may present quite a challenge. But in the following pages you will find plenty of sound, practical advice to help and reassure you in your all-important quest.

Making the Right Choice

Cats and other pets

Before you and your family choose a cat or kitten, you will need to take into consideration your existing pets, if any.

• If you have a dog, you will need to introduce your feline friend with caution. The dog may well feel inclined to protect his territory from an alien-smelling animal. He might also become jealous of the newcomer.

• You already have a cat? A cat who is used to having it all his or her own way in your home will not take kindly to a feline newcomer. In this case, a kitten would be the wisest choice.

• Pet mice, hamsters or rats? These would need to be watched carefully and safely ensconced in their respective cages. If let out indoors for exercise, kitty must go in another room.

• Perhaps you keep rabbits? Cats and kits have very sharp claws so that introductions and any subsequent play-times would need to be supervised.

• Tropical fish will require a lid firmly fixed on the aquarium.

• Caged birds pose another target for cats. Again, supervision or preferably separation will be required if and when the bird or birds are let out indoors.

Home alone?

While one adult cat or, better still, two adult cats may well fare quite happily on their own all or part of the day, it would be most inadvisable — neglectful even — to leave a kitten or kittens in these circumstances. This is mainly because, depending on its age, kittens need to be fed four times a day on average up to eight months old, and these times need to be monitored in the interests of the kitten's welfare. Additionally, the newly acquired kitten, like any young creature, will miss the protective warmth of its mother and siblings, and would pine.

Potential danger?

If an elderly or disabled person is part of your family, you would need to consider the temperament and/or type of feline that you take into your home. Kittens are playful and tend to become more so when they spot moving feet, so this could become a danger to the not-so-nimble human. A nicely matured adult cat may be the best choice here.

Children, too, especially at the crawling stage, are vulnerable. A cat's nice furry tail is just begging to be pulled, and he or she could retaliate with tooth and claw. Close supervision is vital.

Kitten or cat?

Kittens are playful, often boisterous and need constant supervision. While the mother cat has given basic litter training to her offspring, further training after it reaches its new home will be necessary. Often small mistakes occur and will need to be mopped up. These minor incon-veniences are part and parcel of kitten ownership, but with careful and gentle training your kitten should soon be litter-trained. Cats are well-known for their clean and hygienic habits!

Adult cats are, of course, more settled in their ways than a kitten. They are generally quiet, sleep a lot of the time, require feeding about twice a day, should be reliably litter-trained and will not need constant supervision. A bonus will be when you discover that deep inside your adult cat, a playful kitten is straining to get out!

Your ideal cat – points to consider

Pedigree
• Quiet/active
• Longhaired/shorthaired
• Male/female
• Is it your intention to breed?
• Do you want to enter your cat for shows?

Mixed breed
• Quiet/active
• Longhaired/shorthaired
• Male/female
• Neuter or spay since this is not a breeding animal
• Often very attractive; could be entered for shows

Non-pedigree
• Quiet/active not an option
• Temperament not as predictable as with pedigree or mixed breeds
• Male/female
• Neutering or spaying is essential

Your Questions Answered

Q: Ideally, I would like a kitten to be a companion to my adult spayed female cat. Is this wise?
A: Your adult female would accept a kitten as a companion more so than she would an adult – especially so since she is spayed.

Q: Would you recommend my getting two young tom kittens? We have no other cats in the household.
A: No problems with two young toms if you get them both at the same time and if you have them neutered at the earliest possible stage. Your vet will advise you on this.

Q: I would like to give a rescued cat a home. We already have three pedigree show cats. Would they all get on together?
A: Three established cats may not accept a totally different-smelling individual which probably, as a rescued or abandoned cat, already has certain behavioral problems or at least is very wary of new environments. Not recommended.

Q: I have been feeding a lovely tabby who comes to my door on a regular basis. She looks well-fed but always seems to be hovering round my back yard. Shall I claim her as my own?
A: A contentious issue and the answer is no. Put advertisements in local shop windows with a photograph if possible; contact local rescue shelters and the police station to find out if anyone has lost a cat. Try your friendly local radio station – they are often pleased to mention lost and found announcements for free. Only after every possible avenue has been explored should you take the cat in. Otherwise, you could find yourself looking at a court summons, no matter how irresponsible the original owner is seen to be.

Q: I am partially disabled and would like a feline companion. Is this a good idea?
A: Yes. A well-adjusted adult, preferably a non-pedigree, would prove to be the ideal companion, if you feel you could cope with feeding and litter-box routines. Your cat would self-groom or benefit from a little light hand-grooming from yourself.

Q: I am a lone flat-dweller, I work all day but would love to have an elegant – and friendly – pedigree cat to come home to. Would this be a wise decision and if so, what breed is recommended?
A: Some cats are better able to adapt to flat-dwelling than others. Of the pedigrees, British Shorthairs, the Russian Blue, Angora and Burmese are probably the most suitable. Foreign and Oriental types as well as the Siamese, Abyssinian, Maine Coon and Norwegian Forest Cat are quite lively and would not be happy home alone all day. All cats need interactive stimulation in lesser or greater degrees and you would need to provide this whatever your choice of breed. Why not have two young adults to keep each other company?

Q: I would like to have a cat but I am pregnant. Should I wait until after the baby is born?
A: This is not an easy decision to make. If you acquired a cat now, quite naturally, he or she will most likely become jealous of the baby when it arrives. Your attention, again quite naturally, will be directed towards the baby and the cat will not like this. Behavioral problems such as inappropriate toileting and spraying – even with a female cat – will ensue, and the aggrieved cat may leave home altogether. Pregnant and nursing mothers should always wear household gloves when emptying and cleaning litter boxes – these should be secreted away from babies at crawling stage. With careful management babies and cats can survive together. But why not wait instead until your baby reaches three or four years of age and then get a cat?

Q: My cat has recently died and I am undecided whether I should have another or not. Sometimes I think yes; other times I think I am being disloyal to my much-missed feline friend. What should I do?
A: Perhaps you should wait until you definitely know what you want. It would be unfair to take in another cat while you are still grieving for your last one. Take some time to think about this decision. You will know when the time is right.

Domestic Cat Types

Coat types

The Shorthair This coat type may be plush and springy as in the British Shorthair, short and loose-lying as in the non-pedigree tabby types and of a fine, smooth velvety texture as in the foreigns and Orientals, e.g. Siamese, Singapuras, Havanas and Bombays.

The Semi-Longhair A coat type which can be medium to heavy with a profuse ruff as in the Maine Coon, or as in the Norwegian Forest Cat which is similarly ruffed and feathered but double-coated with a tight undercoat shed in summer and a water-resistant topcoat. Silky, flat-coated semi-longhair cats include the Balinese, usually called the "longhaired" Siamese, the Turkish Van and the Angora. The Somali is known as the longhaired Abyssinian but is, in fact, a semi-longhaired cat.

The Longhair Longhairs are of Persian Longhair ancestry. These can be non-pedigrees, hybrids or of pedigree status such as Persian Longhair, the Chinchilla Longhair, Golden Persian Longhair and Colourpoint. The Ragdoll, which has Persian in its ancestry, has a soft, medium-long coat.

Coat patterns

The four main coat patterns are:

Agouti This consists of each hair having three bands of color – cream nearest to the body, then a greyish or ruddy brown and a darker tip. This can be seen in the Abyssinian and tabby coat patterns.

Tabby patterns These comprise the traditional swirling classic pattern, the mackerel with finer, more precise, tabby markings and the "spotted" tabby coat which is a mixture of swirls and spot-like "rosettes." The marbled tabby pattern is less commonly seen and occurs in some small exotics and in the pedigree Bengal.

Tortie or Cameo Tri-coloured coat patterns show a mixture of black and red on white. Diffused throughout the coat, there can also be a fiery mix of totally black and red, or tortie patches of red and black in varying sizes on a white coat. Another variation shows separate "flat" patches of red and black on white. This is called the cameo coat pattern.

Self The body color remains the same throughout. The self coat pattern is seen in many pedigree cats and in black, white and blue (grey) non-pedigree cats.

Eye colors

Eye color in all cats is generally linked to coat color and pattern and falls into three categories: yellow-toned, green-toned and blue. The randomly mated wild and/or feral cat mainly shows a range from amber to hazel to dark copper colored eyes.

Some pedigree cats, in addition to having eye colour linked to coat color and pattern can, via selective breeding, also have odd eyes, one being blue and the other orange. All kittens are born with blue eyes.

Eye types

There are three basic eye shapes in domestic cats today:

The original wild cat eye – open, alert and ready for action and seen to best effect in our tabby non-pedigrees.

The almond-shaped Oriental eye, such as that seen in cats from S E Asia and typically demonstrated in the Siamese and the Korat. Abyssinians and Oriental/foreign type cats with their more modified almond eye shape are also in this category.

The flat, round eye in the shallow socket as seen in the Persian Longhair type.

Body types

There are three basic body types or shapes.

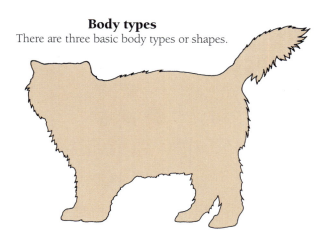

1 Fairly solid, totally functional loose-limbed body of the non-pedigree and/or feral cat with round head and medium pointed face.

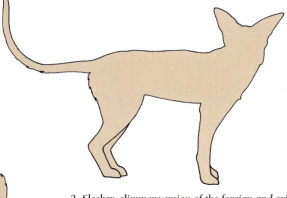

2 Sleeker, slimmer version of the foreign and oriental, with triangular-shaped head, strongly pointed face and a long whip tail.

3 Medium-sized, more moderate adaptation of both 1 and 2, this type having a less stocky body but similar head shape to 1 and the slender legs of 2.

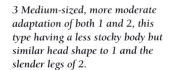

Other coat patterns

Chinchilla Each hair is a lighter shade nearer to the body and is tipped with a corresponding darker colour.

Bi-color Comprising one particular colour patched on white.

Pointed Any cat carrying the Siamese gene for colour confined to the points, i.e. ears, mask, feet, legs and tail.

Van coat pattern Applies to the typical Turkish Van cat, i.e. color confined to the ears and partially to the face, with patches of the same color to the body and totally to the tail.

Birman coat pattern The Siamese gene for color confined to ears, mask, legs and tail, but with white.

Ragdoll coat patterns Pointed as in the Siamese, Bi-colour with large patches of color on white and the Mitted where points are present except on the feet.

Choosing a Breed

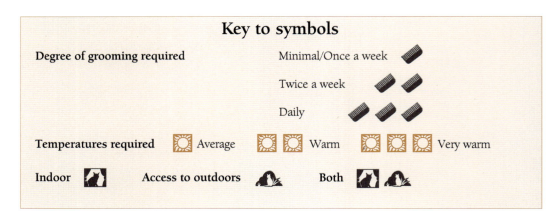

Breed	Coat	Character/Temperament	Needs			
Abyssinian	Shorthair	Lively; athletic	🪮	☀	🐱	🌿
Angora	Semi-Longhair	Quiet; affectionate; gentle	🪮🪮	☀	🐱	
Asian, inc. Burmilla	Shorthair	Intelligent; loyal; lively	🪮	☀	🐱	🌿
Tiffanie	Semi-Longhair	Graceful; intelligent	🪮🪮	☀	🐱	🌿
Bombay	Shorthair	Lively; good companion	🪮	☀	🐱	🌿
Balinese	Semi-Longhair	Graceful; quiet; charming	🪮🪮	☀	🐱	
Bengal	Shorthair	Agile; athletic; intelligent	🪮	☀	🐱	🌿
Birman	Semi-Longhair	Playful; enjoys company	🪮🪮	☀	🐱	🌿
British Shorthair	Shorthair	Sturdy; intelligent; good pet	🪮	☀	🐱	🌿
Burmese	Shorthair	Active; playful; intelligent	🪮	☀	🐱	🌿
Chinchilla Persian Longhair	Longhair	Glamorous; docile; friendly	🪮🪮🪮	☀	🐱	
Colourpoint	Longhair	Active; affectionate; intelligent	🪮🪮🪮	☀	🐱	
Cornish Rex	Shorthair	Athletic; extrovert; people-friendly	🪮	☀	🐱	🌿
Devon Rex	Shorthair	Dainty; mischievous; lively	🪮	☀	🐱	🌿

Breed	Coat	Character/Temperament	Needs
Exotic	Shorthair	Gentle; alert; good companion	
Korat	Shorthair	Sweet; gentle; quiet	
Maine Coon	Semi-Longhair	Active; needs exercise	
Manx	Shorthair	Good hunters; playful	
Norwegian Forest Cat	Semi-Longhair	Active; enjoys climbing	
Ocicat	Shorthair	Gentle; playful; friendly	
Oriental S/h	Shorthair	Lively; energetic; enjoys company	
Persian L/h	Longhair	Sweet; affectionate; relatively active	
Ragdoll	Semi-Longhair	Quiet; intelligent; playful	
Russian Blue	Shorthair	Gentle; quiet; polite	
Scottish Fold	Shorthair	Friendly; likes people	
Siamese	Shorthair	Talkative; lively; inquisitive	
Singapura	Shorthair	Loyal; quiet; affectionate	
Snowshoe	Shorthair	Alert; friendly; playful	
Somali	Semi-Longhair	Playful; gentle manner	
Sphynx*	Hairless	Outgoing; people-friendly but dislikes excessive petting	
Tonkinese	Shorthair	Trusting; devoted; inquisitive	
Turkish Van	Semi-Longhair	Charming; affectionate; enjoys swimming	

Virtually hairless but with a fine down on some parts of the body, the Sphynx requires wiping with a soft cloth to remove dander from its suede-like skin.

Where to Go?

Breeders

If your choice is a pedigree cat to be used for breeding and/or showing or simply as an aristocratic pet, your first step is to contact a breeder. You will find breeders' names and telephone numbers in the specialist cat magazines. Representatives of breed and/or regional cat clubs could also offer help and their contact details can be found in the specialist cat press.
• How about a rescued pedigree cat? Most breed clubs have a rescue or welfare section which deals with rescued and abandoned pedigrees.

If your choice is a non-rescuee, you will have located several breeders of your preferred breed and have made appointments to view the cat or kittens in their home environment. But please, in the interests of hygiene and eliminating the risk of cross-infection, do not visit more than one household on the same day.

Animal shelters

These are often the source of a suitable cat or kitten, and a rescued or abandoned cat or kitten from a shelter will have had the advantage of a veterinary overhaul and treatment, if necessary. Factors to consider in giving a home to a rescued cat are that a) it may not be litter-trained b) it may have existing behavioral problems which could be the reason for its rescued state c) a rescued cat or kitten is an unknown quantity –

you have no idea how it may react to your own home environment.

Both the main rescue shelters of charitable status which accept most domestic animals and those dealing with only cats and kittens have branches in most areas. Your local telephone directory will list contact numbers. There are also smaller charities, often desperately relying on public funds.
• A donation of your choice is often gratefully accepted by most charities in return for a cat or kitten.

Veterinary surgery

Almost every veterinary surgery will carry "homes wanted" notices for domestic animals including cats and kittens. These may be pedigree and/or non-pedigree cats and can be the result of an unwanted litter, an owner's death or simply an inability to keep the cat any longer. One advantage in obtaining a cat or kitten in this way is that the advertiser has probably been a client of the vet concerned and is, therefore, known to the practice.
• How much? A fee may be involved, but often "free to a good home" is the only requirement.

Friends, neighbours or farm

This can often be a most satisfactory method of obtaining a pet cat or kitten. You know the previous owner and also probably, in the case of a kitten, the

kitten's mother. The danger is, in the case of an adult cat, that your newly acquired friend may fail to recognize its new home and/or divides its time between the two!

Farm kittens can grow into independent, self-sufficient cats and generally maintain good health throughout their lives. They will tend to be free roamers and good mousers.
• How much? Cats or kits from friends, neighbors or the local farm will probably be free.

Paperwork

Pedigree: At the time of collection of your cat/kitten (at not under 12 weeks and preferably 14 weeks old), the breeder should give you your cat or kitten's pedigree certificate showing at least four generations of antecedents; its registration certificate; certification to show that necessary vaccinations have been given at nine weeks and boosters given at 12 weeks. These, typically, would be against feline calicivirus, feline herpesvirus 1 and feline leukaemia virus. You should also receive the "transfer of ownership" form, a diet sheet and a basic list of do's and don'ts for your chosen breed.
Non-pedigree: Some rescue shelters could ask you to fill in a form answering basic questions regarding your home and circumstances, to check that you have chosen the right cat to suit your lifestyle, and to make sure that your home is a suitable one for the cat in question to live in.

Choosing a Kitten

• Ears should be clean – ensure there are no discharges and black debris within the ear which would indicate ear mites

• Eyes should be clear, bright and free from discharge, with no "hawes" (third eyelid) showing

• The inside of the mouth should be free from sore gums and/or infection; clean white teeth and pleasant-smelling breath are also essential

Sexing the kitten

Invariably, the breeder will have sexed his or her kittens. However, sometimes the sexing of certain kittens can be difficult.

Female

anus
vulva

Male

anus
testes
penis

• Part hair to check for signs of parasites and "flea dirts" (small dark specks adhering to the fur)

• The kitten should be well-nourished – you should just be able to feel the rib-cage; the stomach should not enlarged (a possible indication of worms)

• Coat should be smooth and glossy, and the skin pink, clean and free from spots or sores

• The kitten should be free from diarrhoea and "clean" under the tail

Preparing for Your Cat

Prepare a checklist before bringing home your cat or kitten to ensure that you have the basic necessities in readiness. In addition to the main items in your "cat and kitten care kit," have plenty of paper towels in stock for possible mopping-up operations. You could also have handy one or two lightweight toys, such as a small ball or catnip mouse. And of course, do not forget the cat or kitten food!

Forward planning

In the excitement of saying "welcome home" to your new kitty, it may be as well to spare a few thoughts beforehand as to where he or she is going to eat, drink, use the litter box and sleep. Presumably your kitchen or utility room will be the best place for these activities, so it is a good idea to make sure that your cat's equipment does not get in the way of normal family routines and activities such as cooking and mealtimes.

• Place the cat box or bed under a table, out of the way of rushing feet and giving the cat a chance to get some undisturbed shut-eye.

• Food and water dishes should also be placed in an out-of-the-way place.

• Place food and water dishes within fairly easy reach of the litter tray but not in close proximity. Cats are extremely hygiene-conscious and prefer to eat away from the litter box.

Cat and Kitten Care Kit

cat carrier: *made of wicker with a rigid wire front-opening door – essential for visits to the vet or travelling in the car*

cat basket: *warmly padded with a blanket and not too high-sided for a kitten*

food bowl: *preferably heavy-duty ceramic or plastic with wide, non-spill base*

water bowl: *ceramic or heavy-duty plastic with wide, non-spill base*

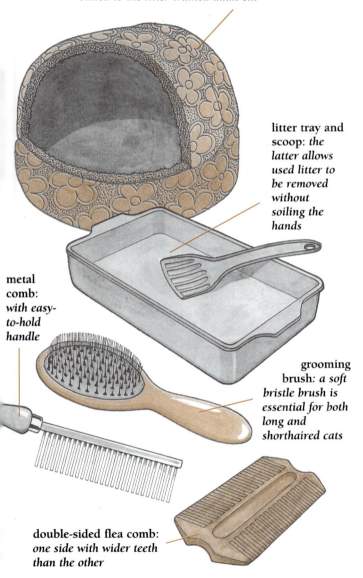

cat cosy: *should be made of padded fabric (can be fake fur-lined) and washable – better suited to the litter-trained adult cat*

litter tray and scoop: *the latter allows used litter to be removed without soiling the hands*

metal comb: *with easy-to-hold handle*

grooming brush: *a soft bristle brush is essential for both long and shorthaired cats*

double-sided flea comb: *one side with wider teeth than the other*

Danger zones

Naturally you will want to take every precaution to keep your new friend out of danger. One way is to ensure that he or she is not allowed out of doors unsupervised to roam at will. Small, dark places hold an untold fascination for both cats and kittens, and while owners worry themselves sick about their "missing" furry friend, said friend can stay secreted away for hours and suddenly and nonchalantly appear at feeding time! With newly acquired kittens and cats, keep outer doors closed at all times and place large notices on these doors to all the family: "Keep closed – on pain of death!!!" However, both in and out of doors serious potential danger lurks. See pages 40-41 for more information on keeping your cat safe.

Bringing Your Cat Home

The journey

Collect your cat or kitten in its new carrying basket complete with blanket. In the case of a kitten, a hot-water bottle partially filled with hot – not boiling – water and well-protected and wrapped in a towel placed under the blanket will be appreciated. Follow these guidelines to help ensure a trouble-free journey home.

• Ensure that the cat's former owner feeds your new friend at least an hour before you take it home. This way, there should be no "accidents" on the journey.

• If possible, cover the cat carrier with a blanket or cloth. This will reduce the stress of travelling. Also, if you are travelling by car, it will reduce the possibility of the cat being car-sick.

• Talk quietly and reassuringly to your cat on the journey. This will comfort it and help to reduce the stress of this new experience.

• Put one of your kitty's new toys in the cat carrier. This may divert the cat's attention and keep it occupied on the journey.

• Ensure that the cat carrier is steady – preferably on the back seat if in a car – to avoid it and your cat sliding about or toppling over.

First introductions

These should be dealt with very carefully, one a time and with great sensitivity. At the first sign of distress on the part of your new cat or kitten, stop and begin again when it has calmed down. In any case, introductions should not be forced on the new cat. When it becomes more familiar with its new territory, kitty will gain confidence and feel much more able to cope with the stress of learning to live with strangers.

Controlled introductions are best. Take the case of meeting the family dog – it would be best to leave the kitten in its carrying basket so that if it becomes frightened it can retreat into the comforting darkness. The dog can then briefly sniff out the newcomer's scent and become familiar with it.

Follow these simple guidelines to secure your new feline's comfort and safety:

• Give the cat or kitten its own space, e.g. a covered play-pen.

• Make sure the cat or kitten is safe and secure at night when everyone has gone to bed. Surprise attacks from the family dog could be fatal.

• Allow the familiar travelling basket in which you brought home your cat to be available at all times during the first week.

• Make sure that a clean litter box is available at all times.

• Do not force your cat to play when it would rather go to sleep.

• Do not allow the family dog to play with the cat's toys. Cross-infection could occur.

The first week

At 12-14 weeks old, a kitten should need three meals a day. If it appears to be hungry, keep it on four. You will know when it is ready to go onto three meals. An adult cat will need two meals a day with perhaps cat treats as an extra. Fresh water should be available at all times.

Do not allow your new kitten outdoors until it is 6-9 months old. Even then, the outside area must be cat-safe (see pages 40-41). In the case of a new adult cat, do not allow it outdoors for at least three weeks and again only then into a safe area. Make sure that other household pets and/or small children do not intimidate the newcomer.

Be prepared to bond with your cat or kitten – play kitty games with it and allow it to climb onto your lap. Keep to a routine in all things, including grooming. Whether cat or kitten, your new friend should fit in with the daily routine of you and your family, not the other way round.

Handling and Stroking

How to hold a kitten

The kitten may be picked up and held in a similar manner to the adult cat. As a smaller animal, the kitten can also be nursed like a baby, lying in the crook of your arm with all four of its little paws in the air. Ensure that the backbone is not cramped and can still be used of the kitten's own free will. The spine is very flexible, but can easily be injured. Always be aware that a kitten's baby bones are soft and can be damaged, unwittingly, through pressure when handling.

How to pick up a cat

So that your cat feels secure when being picked up, do this in a firm yet friendly way with no sudden movements. Talking in a quiet, reassuring way, place your left hand directly under the foreleg. Raise the cat's body slightly and with your right hand lift the cat's hindquarters, with the tail tucked under the body, up and into your arms. If there is resistance from the cat, maneuver your left hand so that the forelegs are restrained between your thumb and four fingers.

Stroking

The therapeutic value of stroking to both cat and owner has already been explored (see pages 6-7). Stroking is also a well-known method of grooming the shorthaired cat – it encourages the natural oils to give a healthy gloss to the coat. Tactile stroking is a "comfort" action – it reminds the cat of maternal grooming sessions. Though a "learned" rather than a natural response in the adult cat, it brings a feeling of comfort and security.

• The cat's stomach is one area NOT to stroke. It arouses instinctual feelings of aggressive arousal.

• Run your hand from the top of the nose, between the eyes, over the forehead and down the back of the skull. This is very soothing for the cat, which will encourage you by pushing its head upwards into your hand.

• Allow your hand to gently straddle across the lower back and feel carefully between the haunches. Clues to intestinal problems can be gleaned this way, e.g. the presence of roundworms, and the cat likes it, too!

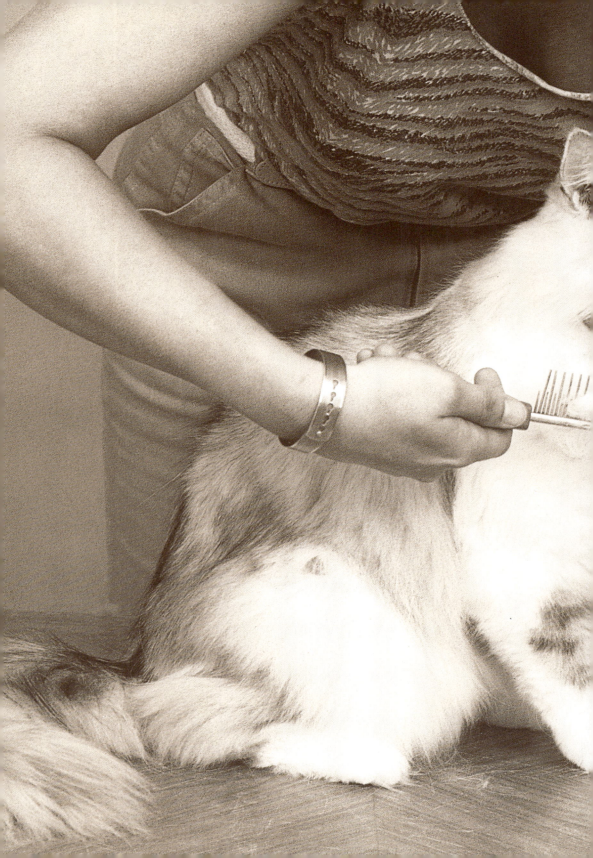

CHAPTER 2

Basic Care

The care and welfare of your cat or kitten is now in your hands. This is not as awesome and difficult as it sounds – a balanced diet, general welfare, health and hygiene can all be achieved with love, attention and sound common sense!

First, remember that you, your family and your cat (plus other domestic animals you may have) all need to live together in comparative harmony. So, early ground rules are essential.

Second, food and nutrition play a large part in competent pet-keeping. A cat that is under-par healthwise will keep the vet busy – and you out of pocket. So, read on for information on how to keep your feline fighting fit and sparkling with good health.

There are also the basic rules of hygiene to consider – essential in maintaining the health of not only your cat but your family and yourself.

Feeding

Equipment

Your cat or kitten will require its own feeding bowl and water bowl. The best ones are of the sturdy, non-spill type, made of glazed ceramic or heavy-duty plastic and must be kept scrupulously clean. Knives, forks and/or spoons used to serve feline meals should be kept separate from those used by the family and/or other animals.

Nutritional requirements

The development from kitten to elderly cat consists of four life stages. Recognize these and you will be halfway to providing the right food for your feline friend.

Kitten: From birth to nine months old, when a kitten is officially regarded as an adult. NUTRITIONAL NEEDS: Nutritious, high-energy foods to build strong bones and maintain good health. Special "kitten" formulas are available.

Young adult: After the age of nine months and until breeding commences. NUTRITIONAL NEEDS: An average balanced diet containing calcium and minerals, generally available from proprietary quality canned foods.

Pregnant/lactating mother and/or the male stud: From one year or sooner to around eight to ten years. Fertile years can differ from cat to cat; from pedigree to non-pedigree cats. NUTRITIONAL NEEDS: Highly nutritious foods complete with

Pawnote: If you have a kitten or kittens and an adult cat – or even dog – feed the kitten(s) away from the older animal, just to give them a chance to get their nose in! Uneasy gobbling of food followed by vomiting could otherwise be the result.

balanced amounts of carbohydrates, calcium/phosphorus and other minerals, fats and oils. Vitamin supplements should only be given on the advice of your vet.

The older cat: The cat, neutered or spayed and/or no longer breeding. NUTRITIONAL NEEDS: Low-carbohydrate, good-quality, nutritionally balanced canned food with a fish oil supplement. Specially formulated diets are available.

How many meals?

Kittens: Up to 16 weeks old – 3-4 meals per day, decreasing to 2-3 meals at six months. By nine months old – 2 meals per day.

Young adult cats: 2 meals per day with a snack of cat treats, perhaps in the evening.

Pregnant/lactating queens and/or stud cats: 2 high-quality, nutritionally balanced meals per day with a milky or lightly vitaminized snack in the evening.

The older cat: 3 or 4 small meals per day, if and when the cat feels like it, including a vitaminized snack.

Special diets

Some manufacturers produce high-quality "natural" diets. These can be expensive. Ask your vet for information on the wide range of medical or age-related formulated foods available. There are also special diet foods for obese cats, cats with kidney problems requiring low phosphorus and low-protein formulas. Special formula foods should be given only on the advice of your vet.

Healthy eyes

Never try to turn your kitten into a vegetarian cat. Cats need meat which contains the vital component, taurine. Taurine is an amino-acid and a level of this in cat food is essential to avoid degeneration of the retina of the eye and also to prevent the heart disease, dilated cardiomyopathy.

dog foods to cats can lead to taurine deficiency.

Basic nutrients

The constituents of canned food comprise:
• **Protein** for muscle development and growth.
• **Carbohydrates** – compounds of carbon, hydrogen and oxygen. Digested and absorbed, these are a source of food and energy
• **Calcium & phosphorus** for healthy bone growth.
• **Natural oils,** e.g. fish oils, promote healthy skin, coat, eyes and mucous membranes

• Other necessary vitamins and minerals often included in smaller proportions are: Vitamins A, C and D, Vitamins B-1 (Thiamine), B-2 (Riboflavin), B-3 (Niacin), B-5 (Pantothenic Acid), B-6 (Pyridoxine), B-9 (Folic Acid), B12 (Cobalamin), Vitamin E, magnesium (ash), manganese, potassium and sodium, and generally selenium. NB: Manufacturers of canned cat foods offer an expertly balanced range of nutrients in their products, which takes the worry of it all away from the cat owner.

Recommended proportions of nutrients

Magnesium, manganese, potassium, sodium and selenium

Vitamin B range

Vitamins A, D, C & E

Protein

Natural oils/fats

Calcium and phosphorus

Carbohydrates

10 cat food facts

• An excess of cod liver oil can cause bone disease.

• An excess of minerals can be dangerous.

• An adult cat needs 20% more protein than a dog.

• Vitamins are essential in the regulation of all the bodily processes.

• Eating too much liver can cause Vitamin A poisoning.

• Siamese cats are particularly prone to Vitamin A poisoning. Keep liver off the menu for Siamese cats, or offer a small quantity once a week only.

• Liver once or twice per week is sufficient for most cats.

• An excess of vitamins A, D or E or of calcium and phosphorus can cause serious health disorders.

• Always read the recommended feeding or dosage instructions on cans, packets or bottles before administering contents. Check labels for a specific magnesium (ash) content. This should average 2-3%.

• A supply of clean drinking water should ALWAYS be available.

Prepared Foods

These can be divided into three categories:

Canned, moist Ideal for nutritious, instant meals

Packet, semi moist: Convenience food in the owner's absence

Packet, dry: Generally fed as a treat, not as a main meal

Canned foods

These can be meat- or fish-based. The main ingredients are meat/fish, cereals, fat, vitamins and minerals, preservatives, water and gelling agents.

Semi-moist foods

Can be fed as an alternative to the canned food, again in meat and fish varieties, or a combination. The main ingredients are cereal, protein, vitamins and minerals, flavoring, preservatives and water.

Dry foods

Again, all meat and fish flavours are available. The main ingredients are cereal, protein, vitamins and minerals, flavoring, preserv-

Serve dry foods in a double dish, with the food in one side and water in the other.

atives and water. These foods are specially dehydrated and drinking water should always be made available with this type of meal.

Fresh foods

Never offer raw meat or fish. It is a good idea to mix finely grated carrots and other root vegetables with the main meat/fish meal, if you can outwit your cat into eating it!

Nutritional treats

Other edible goodies specially formulated to provide extra vitamins/nutrients and delight the cat at the same time are: cat sweets; meat, fish or cheese flavoured cat "treats"; yeast tablets; vitamin-fortified milk-food drops or powder; feline-friendly flavored mineral and vitamin powder to sprinkle onto a main meal.

Cat chews

Just the job to keep kitty's jaws in good fettle – with the added bonus of cleaning the teeth. Never forget that cats are obligate carnivores and that gnawing and chewing is, to them, just part of life's rich tapestry. Cat chews come in meat, fish, cheese and even "mouse" flavors.

Cat milk

A highly nutritious cat milk is available – in waxed cartons, so that you can return it to a cool place after

use. This product is ideal for the food-shy, sickly or elderly cat who will take milk rather than food, and as a supplement for the pregnant or lactating queen. It typically contains vitamins, iron, taurine and lactose.

Liquid refreshment

Water: All cats and kittens need ready access to fresh, clean water at all times. Tap water can be treated with chemicals and your cat may not take to it. If this is the case, the water should be purified.

Milk: Some cats and kittens cannot tolerate milk, since it causes them diarrhea and other intestinal upsets, particularly the foreign and Oriental pedigree breeds. Domestic felines can well do without milk since it is a food, not a means of quenching their thirst.

Green stuff

Believed to maintain digestive balance and to be an emetic in the case of intestinal parasites, cats and kittens enjoy the coolness and pleasing texture of luscious green grass. In the interests of hygiene, it is better to grow your own grass indoors than

allow your cat to nibble at the edges of the lawn, since this could be tainted by pesticides or passing dogs. Cocksfoot grass is recommended and can be planted in containers. Place the container on newspaper or a tea-tray to confine any stray soil.

Catnip

Nepeta cataria or catnip is a garden plant which contains a substance called nepetalctone, similar to the pheromone secretions from cats' glands, in particular the glands on the front and side of the head used in affectionate behavior. Harmless yet allowing a few moments of ecstasy in pussy-cat heaven, dried catnip is used in cat toys, such as catnip mice. Every cat should have one.

Do

• Always clean and if possible sterilize your feline's food and drinking utensils after use. This cuts out possible infection.
• Ensure that pieces of meat are "manageable" for your kitten. Large chunks can choke. Meat which is minced or cut into small, thin slivers is best.
• When you first have your kitten, monitor mealtimes closely.
• Remember that young kittens have small stomachs, so "little and often" is the vital message.

Don't

• Never offer food straight from the refrigerator. Food at room temperature is best.

• Never offer lamb or poultry bones or skin to your cat or kitten. These bones are brittle and can splinter.
• Never leave food down after your cat or kitten appears to have finished eating.

Fussy feeders

It is best to educate your cat's palate right from the start and insist on it taking in a wide variety of tastes and textures. Offer a nutritious menu of small, tasty meals. If these are not eaten immediately, take them away. Cats soon realise that if nothing else is forthcoming, it might be best to eat what is on offer while it is still available! Check with your vet that your cat has no allergies.

Obesity

Greediness – or illness? If in doubt, check with your vet.

Kittens are seldom "fat." An adult cat should not put on weight if it is on a sensible diet and has sufficient exercise. In the elderly cat, an increase in years is no excuse for an increase in girth. Generally, cats are not greedy animals. However, weight gain at any age, particularly when accompanied by lethargy, merits veterinary investigation.

Refusing food

If your cat begins to refuse food, seek veterinary advice. Poor appetite when recovering from, say, cat flu can be revived by giving small, tasty meals with a pungent smell and/or taste, e.g. mashed sardines or pilchards. But there are other reasons for a cat to suddenly refuse food, for instance, a blockage/foreign body in the throat or esophagus, so seek veterinary help immediately.

Training Your Cat

House training

Kittens are given basic litter training by their mums from the time they start to venture out of the nesting box. Cats and kittens are instinctively hygiene-conscious, so you could say that they have the basic urge to urinate and defecate in one particular place rather than at random throughout their (your) territory. So, litter training a kitten is not difficult since you will usually have the kitten on your side.

3 steps to litter training

1. Five or ten minutes after each meal (gauge the time it takes for kitty's digestive system to work), gently place the kitten into a clean litter box.
2. Allow the kitten to settle down (it may take a few minutes for the bowels to work). If it tries to wander off out of the litter tray, carefully return it to the right spot, stroke it gently

and make encouraging noises.
3. On completion of toileting in the kitten's own time, a little cleaning-up might take place. Tell kitty what a good little boy/girl he or she is and encourage him/her to climb out of the litter box.

Litter trays

Two types of litter tray are available – the straightforward "open" litter tray and, for the cat or kit who likes to do things in private, the covered tray. For adult cats, a large-sized, high-sided tray is best. For easy access, kittens need a medium-sized tray.

Types of litter

Fuller's earth: Based on natural clay; dark grey and heavily grained; will leave pawmarks on your kitchen floor.
Lightweight, absorbent: Convenient to carry; light grey and "cleaner" to look at; less likely to "track" onto the floor.

Re-usable: A non-absorbent litter which is washable.
Wood-base pellets: Good for absorbing liquid waste.
Paper-based pellets: A less common, though more eco-friendly litter. Absorbent and easily disposed.

Cat flaps

In the main, cat flaps swing to and fro, allowing the cat – and hopefully not all its friends – free access to both outdoors and in. Magnetic strips attached keep it closed when not in use, which helps cut out drafts.
• Your cat can have a collar with a magnetic strip attached, allowing easy access through the flap. These are not unique, so beware – your home could end up looking like Cat City.
• There is the standard, easy to install, inexpensive cat flap with no locking device.
• A more expensive version features a locking device, enabling you to decide when your cat stays in and its friends stay out!

Cat-flap training

Keep training times to those between-mealtime moments when your cat is getting just a little hungry. Have on hand a saucer of delicious, flavorsome food and place this on the outside of the door. Gently encourage your cat to push his head through the cat flap. To return, cunningly place the food on the inside. Following a couple of successful attempts of going out and coming in, unscathed, cut out the food lure.

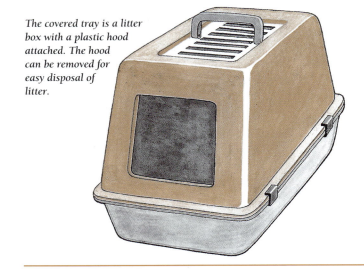

The covered tray is a litter box with a plastic hood attached. The hood can be removed for easy disposal of litter.

Lead Training

Collars and leads

A comfortable, easy-fitting, lined cat collar is ideal. If you can run two fingers under it quite easily when it is fastened, then the collar is not too tight. Check that the collar you buy has an elasticated section – this will ensure that the cat can escape if the collar becomes caught up.

There are a wide range of collars available, and some are impregnated with flea repellent. When grooming, check that the collar has not caused irritation to your cat's skin.

Harnesses

Special cat harnesses are recommended for lead-training your cat. Fitting comfortably over the shoulders and under the ribs, they offer a firm yet gentle restraint. Leads are made of leather or cord and are attached to a ring on the top/back of the harness.

Tags and bells

Identification tags on a cat's collar, either engraved on a disc or secreted in a small tube, are essential for the cat used to going outdoors. Cats that stray can be returned home if they can be identified. A bell attached to the collar is also useful to warn unwary birds of the cat's approach.

Walking on a lead

Unlike dogs, the independent, free-spirited cat does not adapt naturally to lead-training. However, certain varieties, such as the Oriental and foreign breeds, take to it better than others.

1. Training sessions for beginners should be short, starting at five minutes at the most for the first six times and only once per day. As soon as kitty's interest flags, stop and start again another time. As an incentive, food rewards such as cat treats can work.

2. It is best to start lead-training early, at kitten stage if possible. At first, this may be met with refusal, but with gentle persuasion, kitty may walk a few steps with you. Be lavish with praise for even the smallest effort!

3. Start lessons by letting the lead lie loosely, then gradually pull it taut to restrain movements ever so slightly. On gaining confidence, take your cat or kitten for a short walk each day in a quiet spot. Later on, you can try somewhere busier.

The "pull" on the lead in this position is quite comfortable for the cat

The Well-Mannered Cat

Why problems occur

Each type and breed of cat has its own nature and requirements, and its own way of expressing its frustration if these are not met. The latter results in what we imagine to be "naughty" behavior. No cat is "naughty" for the sake of causing problems – although some do possess a mischievous streak! The misdemeanors which occasionally occur with our cats are the result of "things going wrong" with their idea of the ideal life.

Troubleshooting

These are the most common problems caused by cats in the home, with possible explanations for their occurrence and suggested remedies.

Inappropriate urination: This means urinating/spraying everywhere except in the litter tray, usually in response to some insecurity or sudden change of, or in, the cat's territory. Perhaps another cat or dog – or new baby – has been introduced to the home? A threat to its former happy secure existence is the most likely cause for the cat to forget its basic rules of hygiene.
Cure: Instil confidence; offer unconditional, friendly comfort to kitty to reinforce your former loving relationship. Close off all targeted rooms, except the one he or she lives in. Never shout or strike your cat when you see those dreaded wet patches. If matters do not improve, ask your vet to refer you to a feline behaviorist.

Shredding carpets and furnishings: Your cat is only trying to strop off those dead claw skins. In the wild, he would use a tree trunk.
Cure: Protect your upholstery, etc. by providing a scratching post (see opposite). Show your cat how to use the post by holding his front paws on the post and make gentle scratching motions with them. Meanwhile, cover or remove old favorite scratching places.

Unpredictable bouts of aggression: If yours was a formerly easy-going cat, there is some basic deep-seated reason for this problem. Insecurity caused by a dominant other animal? Ill-treatment? Frustration or mental illness?
Cure: Whatever the reason for aggression, seek veterinary help to check out possible physical causes. If that does not offer an explanation, consult a feline behaviorist.

Wool-eating/sucking: When you begin to find soggy holes in your woollen clothes, you know that yours is a wool-eating cat – probably a foreign or Oriental type who is lonely, quietly frustrated and/or is missing its mother.
Cure: Hide away all woollen things. Talk to your little friend; give lots of lap-cuddling comfort and reassurance. He or she might transfer its affections to your arm or other bare parts, so keep those covered, too. Consult a vet to make sure there is not a diet deficiency. If not, talk to a feline behaviorist.

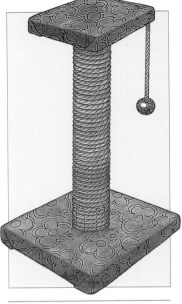

Making a scratching post

1. Obtain a wooden pole or a stout, straight branch, cut to the required height of about 1.2 m (4 ft) high.
2. Prepare two sturdy, good-quality wooden squares, one about 45 cm (1½ ft) square for the top platform and the other about 90 cm (3 ft) for the base. Cover the wood with appropriately sized fine-gauge carpeting, cut larger than the wood to allow for tucking under and tacking down neat "apple pie" corners.
3. Secure the pole to the base with sturdy angle brackets. Attach the top platform to the top of the pole in the same way.
4. Wind an appropriate length of sisal rope neatly round the pole and firmly secure. Attach a dangly toy from the top platform and introduce the post to your cat.

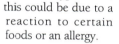

Exercise

Depending on the breed, body type and individual agility, kitty's exercise is all-important. As we humans know, it keeps us supple and fit, and with the release of certain hormones, benefits our mental outlook and well-being. The same works for the cat. Allowed the right amount of exercise, your cat will be happier and could live longer, too.

Indoor workout

Every activity expends energy, and without even thinking about it, the cat instinctively exercises to keep its body fit and supple. It stretches its spine luxuriously as it wakes and it regularly hones its hunting skills as it pounces on toys and small furry mice. The younger cat has moments of frenetic activity, plays tag up and down the stairs and kittens will chase anything that moves. Besides a scratching post, cat "tunnels" and cat aerobic centers, available from pet stores, are ideal for encouraging exercise in the interests of your cat's health and well-being.

Outdoor options

Whether you breed cats and have an outdoor cattery or not, a basic outdoor cat-house in a mesh pen means that your cat can enjoy the great outdoors in comfort and safety while you relax and take in the fresh air. See pages 36-37 for details.

Levels of activity

Age, of course, is an indication of the level of activity required. Kittens race around and play, then just as quickly fall asleep in their tracks. Young adults enjoy their own peak activity hours – usually at around 9 pm, just as you are settling down to watch TV! Elderly cats need less frantic activity, but to keep the circulation going and arthritis and rheumatism at bay, they, too, need a certain amount of gentle exercise.

A healthy cat, contented and at rest after a lively session of hunting and playing.

Lacklustre or hyper?

Lack of energy and an unwillingness to exercise could indicate a sick cat. In this case, early consultation with your veterinarian is crucial. Cats never feign sickness and may have had decreased energy levels for some while before you notice anything out of the ordinary. It is crucial to catch a cat before it sinks into a lethargic state. Cats, particularly, become depressed when they are unwell and often stop eating. If you notice anything unusual, seek out the cause. For instance, if a cat is hyperactive, this could be due to a reaction to certain foods or an allergy.

Outdoor Housing

Types of cat-housing

So that your cat can exercise and enjoy the great outdoors, he or she must be safe while doing so. There are several types of outdoor cat-housing complete with runs which afford both of these pleasures. They can be purchased from specialist suppliers in flat-packed form and professionally erected, or by someone with good DIY skills. Here are just a few examples:

• Specially designed wooden accommodation with runs and with a view to multi-occupancy, e.g. for use when breeding cats or for those requiring rescue facilities

• Stud house facilities (a two-house wooden building that would also accommodate the visiting queen)

• Housing suitable for one or two-cat occupancy, generally designed for the private owner in their back yard or garden

A play-pen

Also available from a specialist supplier is a top-covered, plasticised heavy-gauge metal mesh foldaway play-pen for cats or kittens, suitable for both outdoor and indoor use

10 points to consider

• Ensure your cattery will catch the afternoon sunlight.
• Make sure that any wood stain is cat-friendly. Creosote and tar-based preservatives are poisonous to cats.

Bitumen felt roof

A two-way pet door

• Place food and water bowls on concrete slabs – anything spilled will drain away or dry naturally.
• If this is going to be permanent outside accommodation, heating will be necessary. A low wattage infra-red lamp is ideal.
• Ensure that tree trunks and/or branches have been sanded down to remove rough gnarls and scrubbed to eliminate insect larvae.
• Ensure that the ladder leading to the pen is splinter-free.
• Pre-test all dangly toys so that there are no potential nooses or small loose bits to cause a tragedy.
• Keep only dry food in the run. Damp food and/or meat will

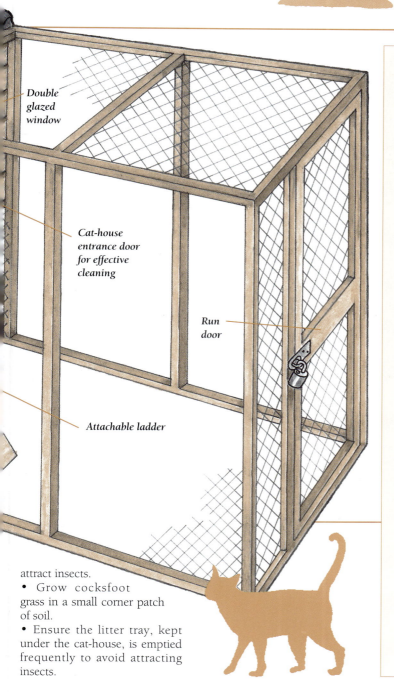

Double glazed window

Cat-house entrance door for effective cleaning

Run door

Attachable ladder

An ideal DIY cat-house and run

Overall size
3.7 m long x 90 cm wide (12 ft 3 in x 3 ft) x 2 m (7 ft) high

Framework
Planed timber

Mesh
Strong, fine-gauge chicken wire-mesh

House
90 cm wide x 90 cm deep x 90 cm high (3 ft x 3 ft x 3 ft)

Construction
Clad with shiplap tongue and grooved boarding. Timber constructed floor. Timber roof with 14 kg (30 lb) bitumen felt

Access
Two-way magnetic pet door

Added features
A scrubbed tree trunk can act as both scratching post and observation post, with a "look but don't touch" taste of the local wildlife! The branches (decorated with dangly toys to catch and bat to and fro) could lead onto "cat" shelves at varying heights and levels erected on one side of the pen.

attract insects.
• Grow cocksfoot grass in a small corner patch of soil.
• Ensure the litter tray, kept under the cat-house, is emptied frequently to avoid attracting insects.

Playing With Your Cat

Play is an essential part of cats' lives – it exercises their bodies and provides an outlet for their predatory behavior. In the kitten it teaches the all-important "life skills" – how to hunt prey, play with it and "kill" it. Play keeps the feline mind and reflexes alert. Play also strengthens the bond between you and your furry friends. When they are not sleeping, cats and kittens of all ages are always ready to play!

Solo games

Catnip mice These are probably the most popular of all the cat toys. As previously mentioned, the aroma is very pleasing for the cat or kitten. Lightweight cotton or fur fabric balls can also contain catnip.

Ping-pong balls Ideal for solo games, since they roll easily and the cat can bat them, attempt to scoop them up and pounce on them as the balls roll about. All good practice for those "life skills!"

Toys on a string All cats like to bat a dangling object – particularly a furry toy mouse, a feather or a brightly colored lightweight ball. Plastic balls which have cut-out designs are not recommended, since these could trap tiny paws.

Games for two or more

Gone fishing Rods with brightly coloured feathers or fish attached to a string are very popular with both cats and kits. You can drag the rod slowly across the floor as a make-

Recommended toys

Soft feathers attached to "fishing" sticks

Mice, balls and small bags stuffed lightly with catnip

Scrunched-up paper balls

Ping-pong balls

Pine cones

Pawnote:

Ensure that all toys you purchase for your cat or kitten are feline-friendly – no small, sharp pieces, no loose beads or mouse eyes or sharp whiskers, etc. Clockwork toys are dangerous since cats can soon tear open the fabric body and quickly expose sharp metal parts. Ensure that stuffed toys are filled only with catnip or soft, shredded fabric – not rice or seeds.

pretend prey, then quickly lift it up into the air.

Fun with feathers Most cats come into contact with birds at some point, and so to heighten the excitement, a small bunch of feathers to tickle your cat with does provide a few minutes of fun! Watch out for those sharp claws, though.

Creative entertainment

DIY hideaway Sturdy cardboard boxes make splendid hiding spots for cats to play in – especially if you have several

Pawnote:

While many cats like to play with wool pom-poms or balls of wool, it is not recommended that cats or kittens are left alone with these. Swallowed strands of wool can cause a serious intestinal blockage – or, at best, playing with wool could be the start of the dreaded wool-eating habit (see page 34).

kittens playing together. Cut off the top four flaps and cut out "doorways" on two or three sides of the box. Turn upside down and let the fun begin.

Step ladders Cats and kittens like to climb, so a small pair of step ladders presents an exciting challenge to the adventurous

feline – especially if you dangle the fishing stick over the top. A few cat treats suddenly appearing on the top step would make a welcome reward, too!

Toy tunnels A cardboard tube, just wide enough for a cat to creep through, is a challenge to the imagination. Treats placed at

one end encourage the intrepid cat or kitten to crawl through to reach them.

Videos for cats Available from pet stores, these usually feature twittering birds and other likely prey – guaranteed to fascinate all felines!

Safety

Home hazards

The kitchen is the room where our comfort-seeking cats like to be. It is also the place where most accidents happen. Washing machines and tumble-dryers should always be checked before use, and check inside cupboards before the doors are closed. Hot plates, ovens and grills, kettles and irons, both while in use and directly afterwards, are interesting to the hungry cat, and unguarded fires or wood-burning stoves with the doors left open seem to hold no fears. Detergents and chemicals of any sort present a potential danger for the questing cat, as well as opened cans. Open windows, too, anywhere in the house are a means of escape, and accident, if these happen to be upstairs windows.

Toxic houseplants

Cats will nibble at plants and these are some common houseplants that are toxic to cats to some degree.
- Amaryllis • Azalea
- Creeping fig (ficus)
- Chrysanthemum
- Dumb vine and others
- Hyacinth • Weeping fig
- Jerusalem cherry (all cherry varieties)
- Mistletoe • Oleander
- Plant bulbs (most)
- Philodendron • Poinsettia
- Sweetheart vine and others
- Umbrella plant • Ivy

Dangers out of doors

The major hazard out of doors is, of course, the open road. Cats cannot be taught how to avoid a road traffic accident. They are aware of the vibrations of oncoming traffic but this is often not enough. Lead-train your cat and he or she will not have to cope with this hazard. The danger of cars does not stop there. Your driveway can be just as lethal. Before you start up the

Toxic garden plants

- Aconitum napellus (monkswood)
- Castor oil plant
- Daffodil and narcissus
- Foxglove • Iris
- Larkspur
- Lily-of-the-valley
- Lobelia • Lupin
- Monkshood
- Virginia creeper
- Wisteria

Indoor F

boiling kettle

open window

washing machine and tumble dryer

open fire

plastic shopping bags

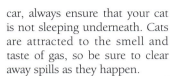

car, always ensure that your cat is not sleeping underneath. Cats are attracted to the smell and taste of gas, so be sure to clear away spills as they happen.

Gardens, both your own and neighbouring, present a potential hazard, too, when insect repellents and slug deterrents are present. Garden ponds should always be securely covered with fine-gauge chicken wire to prevent a drowning. Shut garden tools away.

Other hazards

Any tree whose trunk has been treated with insect repellent is dangerous for cats. Trimmings and clippings from shrubs, hedges, etc. should not be available for cats to chew, since the toxic substances are most active when the clippings have begun to wither and these are often tempting to the cat in this condition. Creosote, flaking paintwork and anti-freeze are also hazards.

Toxic shrubs and trees

- Box hedge • Broom
- Conifers • Hawthorn
- Horse chestnut
- Laburnum • Laurel
- Oak • Privet • Oleander
- Rhododendron
- Forsythia • Thorn apple
- Willow • Yew
- Any tree trunk that has been treated with insect repellent

...ds

pan on cooker

iron on ironing board

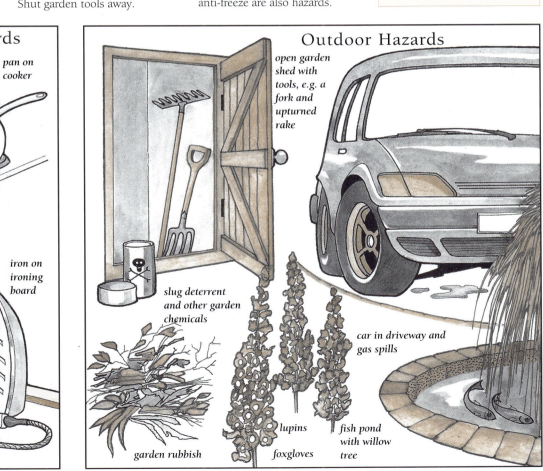

Outdoor Hazards

open garden shed with tools, e.g. a fork and upturned rake

slug deterrent and other garden chemicals

car in driveway and gas spills

garden rubbish

lupins

foxgloves

fish pond with willow tree

Grooming a Kitten

From birth to around eight or nine weeks old, mother cat spruces up her kittens with her rough tongue, "topping" and "tailing" them to keep eyes, nose and mouth mucous-free and under the tail clean and hygienic. After the kittens have eaten a meal, mum can also be seen firmly licking the kitten's anus, to stimulate urination and defecation. This is not only an hygienic exercise, it is also a bonding one, too.

However, by the time you have brought your kitten home – at around 12 weeks old – he or she should be able to self-groom quite adequately. This does not mean to say that kitty's grooming can be left to its own discretion. This is where you, the owner, will need to reinforce the fairly basic tongue-licking routine carried out by the kitten, ensuring that he or she is tangle-free and to deal with the parts he or she cannot reach – ears, for instance.

The kitten coat

It is important to remember that, whether shorthaired, long-haired or semi-longhaired, your kitten still has its kitten coat, with its soft and fluffy fur. Therefore, gentle grooming of the coat once or twice a week is all that is necessary.

Step-by-step kitten grooming

1. Lie the kitten on a flat surface, talk to it quietly and reassuringly and gently hand-stroke down the length of the

The beginner's grooming kit

- A soft bristle brush (not a rubber brush; this is too harsh for a kitten's coat)
- A metal comb, to be used only if necessary
- A double-sided flea comb – probably unnecessary at this stage
- Flea powder specially recommended for kittens
- Pet wipes or cotton swabs

body. Then, following the same motions, introduce the soft brush, talking meanwhile to instil confidence. Bending your head down and looking side-ways up towards the kitten's head, gently blow with your mouth against the lie of the coat. This should reveal flea "dirts" (small, black-looking flecks lying at the base of the hair) and the presence of fleas, if any.

2. If fleas are present, use the flea powder as directed. Meanwhile, continue to brush

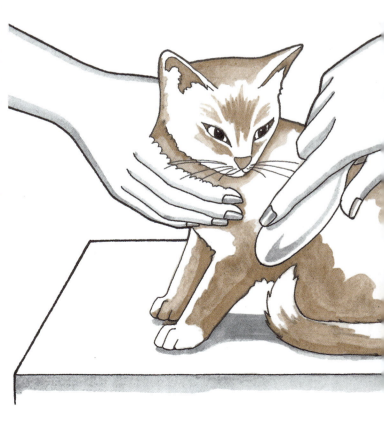

and/or hand-groom, running your hand gently down the back, sides and length of the body. Examine the kitten's underparts. If these need to be groomed, further vocal coaxing will be necessary. Cats do not like their stomachs to be touched, but to avoid unpleasant tangles in the soft hair, this area must be gently groomed.

3. Facing your kitten, take its head lightly between your hands. This way you can check eyes for inflammation or

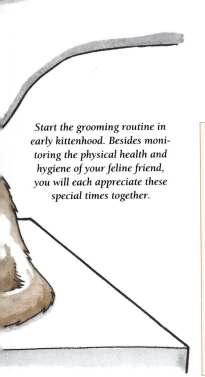

Start the grooming routine in early kittenhood. Besides monitoring the physical health and hygiene of your feline friend, you will each appreciate these special times together.

Grooming routine

- Groom your kitten midway between meals, when the stomach is neither uncomfortably full nor totally empty.
- Choose a time when household chores do not beckon. It is essential that both you and your kitten are relaxed.
- Try to choose the same time each day. This way you can both look forward to this important – and soothing – quality time.

mucous and the nose for mucous or excessive dryness. Using your thumbs, gently persuade open the mouth to check for inflamed gums or teeth problems. Check ears for general cleanliness and in particular for dark debris which would indicate ear mites. Ideally, you should wipe your hands with antiseptic wipes after each stage. Finally, still with kitty's head cupped between your hands, smooth the center of the forehead with an upward motion with both thumbs. This is a pleasant "communications" exercise which will be appreciated.

Cleaning Eyes, Ears and Teeth

You will need:

- Cotton wool swabs
- Cotton buds
- Proprietary brand eye wipes and/or pet wipes
- Tepid, sterile water
- Baby oil

Cleaning the eyes

Place your cat or kitten on a solid surface. Soak a cotton wool swab in the sterile water and with one gentle movement, clean the eye from the outside to the inside. In this way, mucous and/or encrusted debris may be lifted from the side of the eye nearest to the nose. Use a fresh swab if debris still remains. To avoid possible infection being passed from one eye to the other, ALWAYS use a fresh swab for each eye.

Staining

In the case of the Persian Longhair, or any light colored longhair cat which is being shown and when staining is to be avoided, eye-wipes (fresh ones for each eye) gently applied will tend to reduce dark staining to the inner corner of the eyes. Nasal discharge may also be checked at this stage. Sterile swabs or antiseptic pet-wipes will clear away encrusted matter at the nostrils. Check with your vet if this is excessive.

Cleaning the ears

If the inside of the ear flap is dirty, as can be the case with outdoor cats or when there is a normal residue of ear wax, gently wipe clean with a cotton wool swab dampened with baby oil. Dab dry with a clean, dry cotton wool swab. It should be unnecessary to go further into the ear – probing could permanently damage the delicate and sensitive hearing apparatus.

Cleaning the teeth

Prevent oral problems by regular mouth checks and by cleaning the cat's teeth with a special pet toothbrush (or a child's small soft toothbrush) and toothpaste.

Pawnote:

If you discover dark, gritty wax in the ear, consult your vet immediately since this could indicate the presence of ear mites.

Ensure that gums are pink, firm and healthy and that plaque or tartar has not formed at the edges of gums and teeth. Red bleeding gums indicate gingivitis; if treatment is delayed this could develop into pyorrhea – soft, pulpy and painful gums in which teeth become loose and

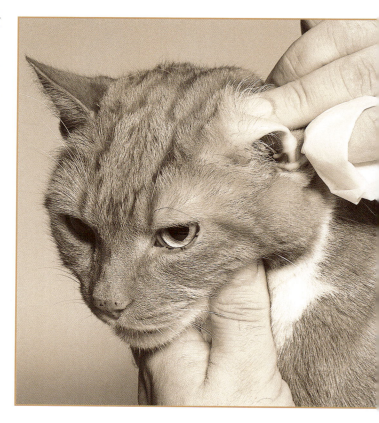

could fall out. Cats do not welcome the daily toothbrush drill, so initiate the kitten carefully and gently with a few seconds of brushing each day. If possible, massage the gums lightly with your finger tip. Cotton buds can remove food deposits after each meal, thus preventing more drastic treatment later on.

Pawnote:

If your cat or kitten refuses food, check its mouth. Even if gums and teeth are relatively healthy, ulcers or other infection may be present.

Clipping claws

Claws are part of the cat's natural defence system and trimming them is rarely necessary, especially if kitty has access to hard concrete floors. If an indoor-living cat is provided with a cat scratcher, again claw clipping may not be necessary. However, examine kitty's claws during grooming sessions and if you do decide to clip them, use the "guillotine" variety of claw clippers.

1. Gently press behind each claw to expose the white (almost transparent) tip and the pink, inner "quick" of the nail. The white tip, as with our own, is dead matter and is all that needs to be cut. DO NOT cut the "quick" since this is living tissue and will bleed if injured.

2. Speak reassuringly to your cat as you position the clippers over the part of the nail beyond the "quick." Squeeze behind the claw quite firmly between your finger and thumb and proceed to trim. Words of praise and favourite cat treats will then work wonders if kitty needs to forgive and forget!

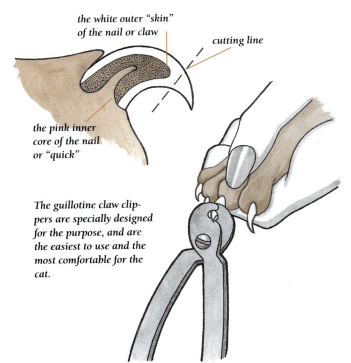

the white outer "skin" of the nail or claw

cutting line

the pink inner core of the nail or "quick"

The guillotine claw clippers are specially designed for the purpose, and are the easiest to use and the most comfortable for the cat.

If you still feel insecure about clipping claws, your vet will do this for you. The secret is to be firm yet gentle, matter of fact and confident. Cats soon detect the slightest hint of nervousness and will rapidly revert to "fight mode."

De-clawing involves the removal of all the claw plus the first toe joint. De-clawing occurs in various parts of the world. In the UK, this is considered to be a cruel and an unnatural practice and vets will not carry out this operation. A de-clawed cat would be disqualified at any UK show.

Grooming a Shorthair

Equipment

- A soft bristle brush
- A rubber brush (for the adult coat)
- A fine-toothed metal comb
- A double-sided flea comb
- A chamois leather cloth or a piece of velvet or silk

Self-grooming may appear to be adequate for the family short-haired cat that is not exhibited at shows. Nonetheless, you will need to take steps to prevent fur balls by making sure that loose hairs are regularly removed from the coat. Fur balls are made up of loose hair ingested by the cat when self-grooming. These can cause intestinal blockages and could require veterinary attention. For the shorthaired cat, grooming is recommended two or three times a week; for the show cat, every other day until a fortnight before the show when once per day is advisable.

Step-by-step grooming

1. Lie your cat on a table or similar flat, solid surface. Smooth kitty's coat with your hands. Using the metal comb, comb in the direction of the fur, away from the head and down towards the tail. Then, comb the against the lie of the fur to ensure removal of loose hair. This is also a good time to check for the presence of fleas. Using the rubber brush, brush down the lie of the coat to remove all loose hair.

2. Turn kitty over so that the stomach is exposed. Gently comb and, if necessary, tease out any rough sections on the chest and underside. Quiet reassurance from you will calm down any natural reluctance on the part of the cat to participate in tummy grooming!

3. Maneuver your cat to a standing position and from top to tail, brush lightly with the bristle

Professional tip

When showing a shorthaired cat, take along your chamois leather or piece of silk or velvet to remove untidy hairs shed while in the show pen. For a light colored cat, talcum powder may be sprinkled onto the coat some 48 hours before the show. Ensure that the talc has not dulled the coat and that no traces are evident on show day. Disqualification may result if powder is evident.

brush. Many owners of short-haired cats hand-groom at this stage. This is done by sweeping the hand from head to tail, thereby encouraging the natural oils in the coat to give a superb shine. Otherwise, brush down from head to tail with a chamois leather or piece of velvet or silk. This also produces a magnificent sheen.

Grooming a Longhair

Equipment
- A stiff bristle brush
- A rubber brush
- A double-sided flea comb
- Baby talcum powder
- Blunt-ended nail scissors
- A wide-toothed metal comb

With the longhaired cat, whether pedigree or non-pedigree, it is most important to maintain a regular 15-minute grooming session each day. This will prevent painful matted hair which may have to be removed under anaesthetic by your vet, if allowed to become too matted. Regular grooming also helps to keep down the presence of fur balls – often an ongoing problem with longhairs. To maintain good relations between yourself and kitty, murmur reassuring words throughout the grooming process!

Step-by-step grooming

1. Again, choose a flat, solid surface on which to groom your longhair. Run the wide-toothed comb lightly along the back of the cat, gently teasing out any minor mats. If you find the coat resists the comb in any way,

hold each portion of hair as you comb to avoid discomfort. This is a good point at which to check for the presence of fleas. Having combed the back, blow against the lie of the hair to detect flea "dirts" (small black-looking flecks lying at the base of the hair). If these are present, treat accordingly.

2. Turn kitty over to reveal the stomach. Proceed with care and caution because this is not only a sensitive area but also the place where the worst mats appear – underneath the "armpits" of the forelegs, between the hind legs and under the tail. If mats are present, lightly sprinkle with talcum powder and tease these apart with the fingers. If completely resistant, the knots may have to be cut away. Avoid nicking the skin by placing your thumb and forefinger between

Professional tip

To enhance the delectable cloud-like appearance of the light-colored longhaired cat, part the hair throughout and lightly sprinkle in talcum powder. Brush thoroughly to remove surplus talc and fluff out the coat, especially around the head and the ruff area, with your hands. For the show cat, do this at least 48 hours before the show.

the scissors and cat. Tease out and comb the remainder of the coat, paying special attention to the "ruff" or "bib" – the heavy fur underneath the chin.

3. Finally bring your cat to a standing position, and using the soft bristle brush, brush out the coat thoroughly to give a healthy, overall sheen.

Bathing Your Cat

Equipment

- Kitchen sink/large bowl or bath
- A rubber mat
- Cat shampoo or baby shampoo
- 2 large rough towels
- A hand-held shower spray, if possible, or an extra bowl containing tepid water

With the shorthaired family cat not intended for showing, bathing should be unnecessary – unless the coat has become particularly soiled. The short-haired show cat should be bathed approximately 48 hours before a show, to give time for the natural oils to return and add a sheen to the coat.

The longhaired cat, whether a show cat or not, does benefit from bathing, since a) the soaping may help disentangle mats and b) the long coat undeniably looks healthier and fluffier after a bath. There will be no necessity to bathe kittens from birth to around 9 months old – soiled parts may be cleaned with dampened swabs.

Shorthair, longhair or semi-longhair cats will all need to be bathed if they suffer from stud tail – a condition which can occur in either sex. Stud tail is caused by over-production of sebum by the sebaceous glands under (the dorsal aspect of) the tail. Careful bathing and veterinary treatment is necessary.

The following bathing sequence for both shorthairs and longhairs, should be carried

out swiftly and with confidence. Ideally, all bar the drying process should be over in three or four minutes!

Step-by step bathing

1. Prepare the sink, bowl or bath by first placing the rubber mat at the bottom and then filling with luke warm water. Test the temperature of the water by dipping in your own bare elbow. The water level should just reach the cat's stomach.

2. Place the cat carefully but firmly into the bath and cup the water in your hand to dampen the whole coat as far as the back of the ears, not forgetting the legs. Do not wet the face – clean afterwards with damp swabs – and ensure water does not enter the ears.

3. Pour two or three capfuls of pet or baby shampoo into your hand and, starting with the back, gently rub into the cat's coat. Sluice with water and

Dealing with problems

Matting With the long- or semi-longhair cat, it is best to cut out severe mats before bathing. The bathing itself will then help the coat to settle down. Try to feather the hair as you cut, but do not worry if jagged edges are apparent. These will soon blend into the coat.

Moulting Bathing is a good idea when the cat is in moult, since this is an excellent opportunity to wash away excess hair.

When not to bathe If your cat is feeling less than well, hold off bathing until he or she is feeling better. As with us all when our immune system is under attack, we are vulnerable to other health problems.

Open sores If your cat has

excema or other skin complaints or abrasions, severe cuts or scratches, avoid bathing or allow wounds time to heal before bathing, unless otherwise advised by your veterinarian. If bathing is recommended by your vet, a special preparation of tea tree oil for pets may be added to the water as a soothing antiseptic. Use as directed.

Upset cat If by any chance your cat takes fright while bathing and becomes unmanageable, quickly wrap him or her in your second, dry towel. Quickly place the towel on the cat's back and wrap it fairly tightly around the legs to avoid being scratched. Hold the cat firmly under your arm until it has calmed down.

smooth the soapy water up and down the legs and under the tail. With your left hand, hold up the cat under the forelegs so that it is standing firmly on its hind legs. Swish more water onto the stomach with your free hand and add more shampoo if necessary. Gently rub into the front area and up and around

Pawnote:

Ensure that only pet or baby shampoo is used. Shampoos for adult humans can be toxic to cats, especially the dandruff-deterrent type. Dog shampoos can also be toxic to cats.

the neck. Do not use too much shampoo, or it will be difficult to remove at the next stage.

4. This is where a shower spray comes in very useful, preferably complete with a wall bracket so that you can have two free hands. Again, test the running water quickly and spray through the coat, taking care to reach into the neck fur, under the legs and the tail. If you have not got a spray attachment, carefully pour out previously prepared water from the extra bowl. Make sure that all soap is removed.

5. Smooth along the body with your hands to remove excess water, then place one of the towels over your cat's body. With a swift, decisive move-ment, lift out the cat onto the second rough, dry towel previ-ously placed on the draining board or table.

6. Towel dry briskly, making sure that all excess moisture is removed. Carry on rubbing briskly until you are satisfied that your cat is totally dry. A hair-dryer can be used to finish off – if your furry friend has no objections! The longhaired coat benefits from blow-drying.

7. Afterwards, kitty will probably settle down to groom itself to regain its own familiar taste and smell. Leave him or her alone to do this for a few minutes, then groom with a soft bristle brush (see pages 46-47).

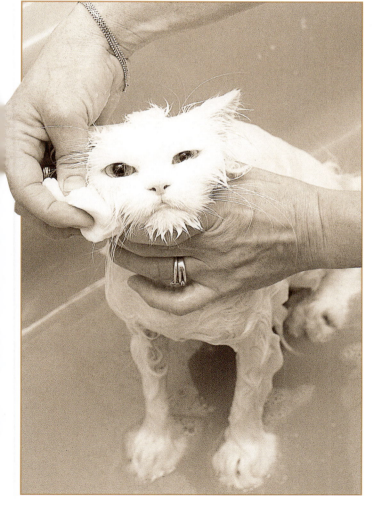

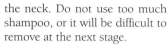

The Travelling Cat

Types of carrier

• Front-opening wicker basket with easy-to-open wide mesh door. Ideal for short journeys to the vet, etc.
• Front-opening heavy-duty plastic carrier, which you can see through and is ventilated – an alternative to the above
• Cardboard pet carriers obtainable from your vet at very little cost – no more than emergency transporters (a determined cat can easily claw its way out of this type)
• Durable non-transparent plastic carrier opening at the side or by lifting up the top; side-ventilated with a mesh frontage for vision – security-minded for both you and the cat and ideal for long journeys such as travelling to shows
• Special regulation flight containers for journeys by air – supplied by the point-of-exit personnel handling the exportation of your cat

Travel by car

Depending on the distance you intend to travel, either of the main plastic cat carriers are recommended (see left). For the long haul, offer food one or two hours before the journey to allow stomach contents to evacuate before starting off. Provide a piece of comfortable, warm and absorbent bedding to place inside the cat carrier. Keep bottled water and a bowl to hand and offer ONLY if required. If the journey lasts for some time, dry cat treats will be acceptable. In any event, to avoid accidents, do not allow the cat to roam free in the car. If he or she sings loud and long in protest at the journey, say soothing things occasionally, while appearing not to pay too much attention to the vocalist! Keep the car ventilated by opening a window slightly, but do not allow the air to blow straight into your cat's face.

Since car sickness is caused by an imbalance to the hearing mechanisms, brought about by the countryside appearing to whizz by at great speed, cover the top and sides of the carrier with a blanket or a cloth, allowing forward vision only.

Rail travel

Usually, your cat will be allowed to occupy a seat next to you when travelling by rail. You will have purchased a ticket for your cat and made sure it is safely housed in an escape-proof cat carrier with a warm blanket. The carrier should be solid-sided, non-see-through and preferably facing the engine in the forward direction. On some railway networks and when travelling unaccompanied, cats are stowed in their carriers in the luggage compartments. Do not offer food immediately prior to the journey.

Sea travel

Consult your vet prior to travelling by sea with your cat. It may be considered advisable to give a sedative beforehand, to avoid distress. Again, food should be offered sufficiently early to allow the system time to eliminate waste matter. If short ferry trips are undertaken quite frequently, your cat may become used to these journeys. Ensure, if yours is a journey on a passenger ship, that your cat is safely contained in its carrier and placed in a quiet corner where it will not slide about and only the minimum of swell is felt, if possible. Ask for special stowage if in doubt about weather conditions.

Air travel

Special arrangements must be made when travelling by air. Consult your vet, who may be able to advise on travel arrangements and certainly will supply the necessary vaccinations and certification to enable you to enter another country with your cat. According to the country you are leaving and/or entering, see governmental specifications and requirements for transporting an animal by air. Often quarantine catteries will handle this aspect of the journey for your cat. They will transport your cat to the airport, safely housed in a special flight container, and will arrange for its paperwork to be inspected at the other end.

Consider how your cat will react to the food, climate and various other conditions in the

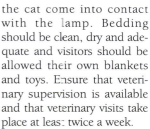

Boarding a cat

Booking

Book early, since good boarding catteries get booked up well in advance. For your own convenience as well as for the welfare of your cat, choose the most suitable cattery nearest to your home.

Inspection

Visit the cattery first before you book. Look out for clean, spacious quarters, adequate "sneeze barriers" between the pens and other contented feline visitors all looking in good condition. Ensure that adequate heating is available. Infra-red lighting is preferable, emitting a low-wattage, continuous heat. Check that heaters are placed out of the way and/or have protective covering should the cat come into contact with the lamp. Bedding should be clean, dry and adequate and visitors should be allowed their own blankets and toys. Ensure that veterinary supervision is available and that veterinary visits take place at least twice a week.

Make sure that kitty's records will be displayed on its cabin door and that details of special food requirements and/or medicines to be administered are available to all members of staff on duty. Also ensure that in case of emergency the telephone numbers of your own holiday venue or of friends or relatives are listed. Meanwhile, you can relax and have a great time on holiday knowing that kitty is also enjoying his or hers, too!

country to which you are travelling. Do not insist on taking your cat to live in another country if it is too old or to nervous to make the journey and/or adapt to another way of life. Find a good home for it before you go.

Quarantine

The rules regarding quarantine for animals entering a country vary from country to country. Contact relevant export and shipping authorities for current information regarding the country of your proposed destination. Generally, quarantine is designed to prevent the spread of rabies – especially applicable to land-locked countries such as those in Europe. Cats have rarely been known to carry rabies.

The Elderly Cat

Signs of ageing

Cats have been known to reach the grand old age of 34, but this is the exception rather than the rule. 15 years is considered a very good age for a cat and anything above that is indeed a bonus. However, in medical terms, a 10 year-old cat is considered to be geriatric.

As the years go by, the ageing cat spends an increasing amount of time asleep. Because of this, many owners find their elderly felines most rewarding companions. No more mad half-hours in the evening; no more rushing up the curtains or energetic tearing apart of furniture. At last, they are much more sensible, know when to keep out of the way, are much more placid and appreciate your company in a quiet and undemanding way.

With the excellent standard of veterinary care and specialist diets now available, many elderly cats show few signs of ageing. They may put on some weight through an unwillingness to exercise, but other than that they can appear to be physically quite fit. Eventually, however, brain activity does slow down and there is some memory loss, irritability and general disorientation. Hitherto good toileting habits will become less reliable and he or she may "leak" while still asleep. But you must understand and make allowances for all these little hiccups as you would with any elderly person.

If you have given a firm foundation of a healthy diet and a sensible lifestyle from kitten through to cat, your elderly feline can now rest assured that your love and care will continue to provide all he or she could possibly need in.

Common problems and ailments

Some of the problems confronting the elderly cat are:

- A lowering of the immune system and general susceptibility to infection
- Mouth disease and subsequent loss of teeth; ulcers and sore throats
- Digestive upsets; the inability of the stomach and intestines to digest food
- Brittle bones and subsequent breakages
- Muscle weakness
- Arthritis in the joints and general stiffness
- Bronchitic conditions; wheezing due to lungs becoming less efficient
- Inefficient breathing means less oxygen to the muscles causing fatigue and sometimes physical collapse
- This can also lead to the symptoms of senility, such as disorientation, behavioral changes and memory loss
- Inefficient functioning of the liver and kidneys
- Problems with the "waterworks," incontinence and edema
- Impaired and/or decreased function of the faculties – hearing, sight, taste and smell
- High blood pressure
- Anemia
- Cancer/tumors

Health checks

Your elderly cat will rest quietly most of the time. This may be because of fatigue or general lethargy, or could it be due to sickness or disease. Being aware of the subtle changes in the habits of your cat can help avoid these problems and by contacting your vet early, you may prevent the deterioration of a health condition. Better still, take your cat along to see the vet on a regular basis to have heart, lungs and blood pressure checked. This way, your cat is in capable hands and you could be saved the expense of more intensive care or even hospitalization.

Life expectancy

It is often believed that a non-pedigree lives longer than a pedigree cat. This is not strictly true, although by reason of its probably hardy, perhaps feral background and self-sufficient lifestyle, the non-pedigree may be tougher and more resilient than the pedigree cat. "Natural" breeds such as the Norwegian Forest Cat or the Maine Coon have a reputation for being hardy animals, mainly because of their ability in their native countries to survive in severe weather conditions. But generally, for the domestic cat who is well-cared for, fed a sensible diet and kept safe from the dangers of the roads, life expectancy, barring accidents and unexpected illness, is on average 12-15 years of age.

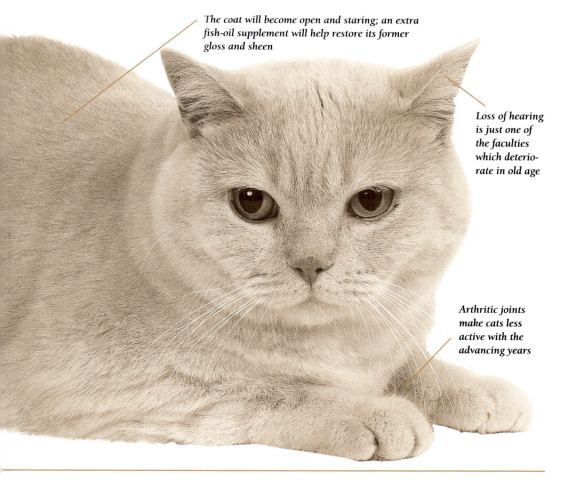

The coat will become open and staring; an extra fish-oil supplement will help restore its former gloss and sheen

Loss of hearing is just one of the faculties which deteriorate in old age

Arthritic joints make cats less active with the advancing years

Care in Old Age

Caring for the elderly cat requires patience and understanding, as well as time. Sometimes puss has difficulty with food and may have to be encouraged or spoon-fed; he or she may be incontinent, so bedding will need to be washed and changed. All this does take extra time, but after a lifetime of happy memories together, perhaps this is the least we can do to ease our elderly pet through the latter part of his or her life.

Feeding

Your elderly cat will need fewer calories to compensate for the decreased use of energy. Weigh your pet on a regular basis on flat scales to ensure that he or she is not gaining too much

> **Pawnote:**
> A tasty meal of sardines or pilchards in oil once or twice a week will not only bring your cat back for more, it will also help to prevent constipation.

and, if so, adjust the calorie intake accordingly. Special diets for obese cats are obtainable from your veterinary surgery.

Always ensure that clean, fresh drinking water is available and make any changes to the diet gradually, offering more tasty, tempting foods to titillate the now not-so-sensitive palate. Food should always be warmed to room temperature. An excess of certain ingredients in canned cat foods, such as protein, phos-

phorus and sodium for example, should be avoided (see pages 28-29 for more information on dietary needs of the elderly cat). Vitamin A, the B range; B1, B6 and B1 and Vitamin E are beneficial, as is zinc in the correct proportion, to boost the immune system. Consult your vet if in doubt. Also, ask your vet for any relevant nutritional and/or dietary update for the elderly cat.

Grooming

Elderly cats become a little lax in their self-grooming habits and so your assistance will be necessary and probably much appreciated. Keep up with your grooming routine of regular brushing to remove dead hairs, topped up by a soothing hand-groom after-

Make a "tent" out of the wool blanket in your feline's cat cosy, basket or box. He or she can snuggle up in there, away from all possible drafts or disturbance!

wards. These episodes will also give you the chance to examine eyes, ears and mouth for possible infection and also the coat for possible flea infestation.

Time to groom

If your cat is a little bit irascible when its reverie is interrupted for a quick groom, observe both its sleeping and its active times and judge when is the best time for you to approach this necessary routine.

Keeping warm

With old age comes a less than efficient circulation. With lack of sufficient blood flow to extremities, a cat of advanced years may suffer mild hypothermia if room temperatures are cool. Cold cats, especially whey they are old, become sluggish and depressed, so ensure that yours is kept in a pleasant, not too hot environment. Prevent him or her sleeping in drafts by providing a padded cat cosy or warm cardboard box and wool blanket to sleep in. A hot water bottle, well wrapped in a towel and placed under a bottom blanket to avoid burns, will provide a much appreciated warmth for the old bones of an ageing cat.

Exercise

Having said that, nothing improves the circulation like a spot of exercise! Invest in a cat scratcher or cat aerobic centre if you have not done so previously. Exercise is also mentally beneficial. As is the case with the human brain, the more the cat's brain is worked, the more plentiful are the connections between brain cells with less likelihood of senility setting in. So make a special effort to play with your elderly cat.

A peaceful end

Regrettably, the time will come when you will have to say your last goodbye to your dear old friend. This will be the hardest moment of all in a relationship spanning probably, if you have been lucky, at least one and a half decades. Perhaps your old friend died in his or her sleep – the best way, we would surely all agree. Perhaps there was a terminal illness, when you had to put aside your own feelings of grief and say yes when your vet advised euthanasia. There is always a time to let go, and you will know when this very special time comes along, when it is kinder not to put off the deed until tomorrow but to say your last goodbye now, today.

Make arrangements to take your cat's body home and then, as soon as possible, decide on your preferred method of interment for your pet's body. This could be burial in your garden; burial in some other wilder spot, by a river or under trees; burial in a designated pet cemetery or cremation, usually at a pet cemetery.

If your choice is a private burial in your garden or in a natural spot, you can create your own remembrance service. Should the more public burial or cremation be preferred, find out the most suitable, and nearest, pet cemetery from specialist cat magazines, your local newspaper or from your vet's notice board. This should be done as soon as possible since an appointment will need to be made. There will be a charge for this service and your pet's remains/ashes will be interred in a suitably sized casket, engraved with a message and your cat's name. In the case of cremation, you will have the small casket or urn either placed in the garden of remembrance or for you to take home.

Chapter 3

Understanding Your Cat

Take the time and patience to understand the nature of your cat, the way its mind works and the reasons why it responds and reacts to certain challenges and situations. Understanding the cat's underlying *raison d'etre*, as you will see, brings its own rewards.

Learning that the cat is, essentially, a solitary hunting animal is the very first step to understanding your own feline friend. It is independent, answers to no individual and its actions reflect more the requirement to satisfy its own needs rather than those of others.

Today's domestic cat, living alongside its human family, will have masked and hopefully, adapted its primal instincts to the unnatural environment of human housing. If nurtured correctly, with loving care and consideration, your pet cat will enjoy a full and happy life. Achieving this blissful state is a two-way compromise for you both, but the end result is well worth the effort and guaranteed to be a rewarding, satisfying and pleasurable experience!

Social Behavior

In any situation where the cat is faced with what appears to itself to be a challenge, it will respond to that situation in either an innate natural feline way or with examples of learned behavior, i.e. ways in which the cat has discovered will help it gain or accomplish a need or requirement. In the pedigree cat, selective breeding generally predicts a particular type of nature. In addition, the breeder will obviously elect to breed cats of good temperament, suitable for the family home and/or for show purposes. That is not to say that the odd rogue temperament does not crop up among pedigrees occasionally, but these are the exception rather than the rule and are often the result of irresponsible breeding or some earlier, unhappy experience.

Non-pedigrees have less predictable natures, their parentage and origins often being unknown. The temperament of hybrids, on the other hand, can be fairly reliably predicted, since these are usually the intended result of cross-mating two different pedigree cats.

Whatever the origin of your cat, however, there will be times when your pet's good manners appear to have been thrown to the winds!

Territorial behavior

The cat's attachment to its territory not only applies to the feral cat, where large areas of countryside are classed as its own, but to the domestic cat within the particular environs of its home or garden. Wherever and whatever they consider to be home ground, the extremely territorially minded cat will protect and discourage other cats and animals from invading it.

The feral cat's territory is marked by "outposts" – points at which the cat urinates or sprays to warn off other individuals. To a certain degree, the same can be said of the domesticated household cat. Spraying or urinating on certain objects in the home reinforces the same message.

Hair along the spine stands on end emphasising size – an automatic reaction of the nervous system

Ears swivel so that they are turned back-to-front

The tail stiffens, hangs low and fluffs out – the nervous system's automatic reaction in the fight or flight response

Guarding territory

Since the domestic cat will ferociously guard its territory (your home), you can understand why careful integration of newcomers to an existing cat's territory is essential. Short, monitored

Eyes become elongated as the head draws back in a threatening posture

Lips curl back to reveal the teeth

The ruff around the jowl area also puffs out when two male (stud) cats fight

exposures are necessary in the first instance until the smell and sight, in that order, of the newcomer becomes familiar.

Signs of aggression

These are easily identified as an arched back with the "hackles" or spinal hair opening up and standing on end; the swivelled, turned back-to-front ears and the curled-back lips showing the teeth. There is also a sudden lashing out of outspread claws – all of which displays aggressive arousal designed to terrify the attacker or trespasser.

Dealing with aggression

Never rush in and interfere with battling cats. This is especially ill-advised with two entire males – warring males mean serious business and their aggression may well be redirected on to you if you intervene. A popular deterrent is a water pistol aimed at the cats' rumps or whatever part of their body presents itself at the time, and may help distract their attention. If not, fling the nearest blanket or towel over the cats and leave them alone – they will soon lose interest in each other in their rush to escape the blanket. They may resume but with less ferocity this time, since the first heat is now over. If they do, clap your hands loudly or resort to the water pistol again.

Minor scuffles

As opposed to the fully fledged battle, there is the comparatively minor scrap, for instance, a

"keep out of my food bowl" or "that's my chair" gesture. This is usually quelled in a common-sense way by a sharp voice command or simply by removing the offender to, say, his or her own dish/chair, thus calming down the affronted feline.

Battle wounds

Torn ears, scratched and bleeding noses and skin and any other injury caused by fighting all need to be disinfected before serious infection sets in. If your cat has been fighting, it is most important to locate the wounds and treat immediately and according to severity.

For superficial wounds, a recommended dilution of tea tree oil is a useful mild antiseptic. Dab this on the wound with a clean swab. Never use antiseptics containing phenol; this is toxic to cats and can be absorbed through their skin. For more serious wounds, consult your vet. If possible, ensure no wounds are missed. Cats can be quite secretive about their hurts, and should you see yours limping a day or two after the fight, check hidden places such as inside legs or paws.

Feline Friends

Cats in a colony, for example two or more cats in a household, can co-habit in a moderately friendly way so long as each recognizes the other(s) and where each fits in the scheme of things. There are times when groups or pairs are particularly amicable, for instance during mutual grooming rituals or when they pile up and sleep together. But there are certain individuals that do not ever seem to hit it off together. Their smell or perhaps some remembered trauma will trigger off an aggressive response. In cases like these, the re-homing of one animal into a more neutral environment is a sensible solution.

Friendlier felines

Spaying, neutering, de-sexing or altering – the removal of ovaries in the female and castration of the male – is strongly recommended in multi-cat households to avoid the unnecessary sexual arousal that entire animals would constantly cause. In the case of a group of pedigree cats used for breeding purposes, separate and adequate housing is necessary. Neutering in cats significantly reduces objectionable behavior, i.e. fighting, roaming, and urinating or spraying, and gives a cat a much more companionable and owner-friendly profile!

Cats and us

Our cat's relationship with us, whether we are male or female, is that of kitten and mother. We

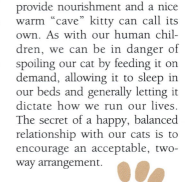

provide nourishment and a nice warm "cave" kitty can call its own. As with our human children, we can be in danger of spoiling our cat by feeding it on demand, allowing it to sleep in our beds and generally letting it dictate how we run our lives. The secret of a happy, balanced relationship with our cats is to encourage an acceptable, two-way arrangement.

Pawnote:

Some animal ethologists feel that parting an animal from its ability to procreate and subsequent natural behavioral patterns is cruel and wrong. But keeping two or more entire domestic cats together in one household and hoping to maintain any semblance of order is impossible.

Sexual Behavior

Sexual activity in cats can occur for some from as early as four months of age. The mating ritual is triggered off when the male picks up the scent of a female in oestrus or in season.

Call of the wild

In the wild, the female obeys nature's command that she should proliferate her species and advertises her fertile condition by vocally informing every male within earshot. While the female cat was anciently branded promiscuous, as per Dianic myth, she is not unnecessarily so; nature is simply urging her not to waste a single opportunity to mate and produce young.

The questing male

From the furthest reaches of his territory, the opportunistic male hears and responds to her call. He sniffs out the receptive female and mates with her. Researching behaviorists have observed that mating can occur some 10-20 times in one day.

Roaming

Apart from answering the call of his hormones and proliferating his own species, whenever he gets the chance, the role of the tom cat in the wild is also to patrol the outposts of his often large territory hunting for food for the female and young, although often she is left to forage for herself. His parental role in respect of his kittens is practically over. Likewise, the domesticated male cat, slipping out through the cat-flap, re-enacts the role mother nature earmarked for him. Unless neutered, and this would significantly reduce the will to roam and repress vital reproductive urges, a male pet cat will carry on tom-catting all over the surrounding neighborhood and beyond.

The missing cat

Even in a well-ordered lifestyle, the most awful thing in the caring cat-owner's life can occur – your cat goes missing. Try to be cool and practical.

1. Search the house thoroughly checking every space you think he could squeeze into. Call his name, rattle his food bowl and open up his favorite, most pungently smelling food. Cats can sleep for hours on end but eventually they will wander back to familiar territory for food.

2. After six hours with no sign, search outhouses, neighbors' sheds and any empty properties. Search yours and neighboring gardens – he could be lying injured under a bush, especially if he has been knocked down by a passing car and attempted to stagger home injured.

3. After 24 hours, contact the police to find out if there has been a road accident involving a cat. Contact your veterinary surgery – they may have given emergency treatment to an injured cat. Call your local radio station – they will often broadcast a help message.

Contact all the local rescue centers.

4. Prepare notices and post on lamp-posts, in local shop windows, supermarket notice-boards, local schools – children are often very observant where animals are concerned – and your veterinary surgery. Contact the police again. Check local train and bus stations.

5. After three days' absence, confirm that neighbours, or even those further afield, have not gone away on holiday and left their garages locked with your cat inside. Telephone rescue shelters again for news of recent stray cats being brought in.

6. Comb the countryside – your cat may have reverted back to the wild. Some pedigrees, Somalis for instance, are known to do this. Investigate any local empty houses again. Post messages on the Internet – many cat clubs and cat-minded people have Web sites.

Still no sign? Stories of cats returning to homeground after two or three years of having left it are not uncommon. Your cat may simply have preferred someone else's home to yours. If so, some old memory may trigger off that strange sixth sense a cat undoubtedly has, and perhaps will guide him back home to you.

Hunting

Whether preying upon small livestock in the wild or the catnip mouse in the sitting room, the cat was born to hunt and its physique and mentality is specifically designed for this lifestyle. When we fear for the fate of wild birds in our garden, we try to stop naughty, cruel kitty from doing what comes naturally to him. We want to believe that "red in tooth and claw" is not where our fluffy fireside friend is at.

A cat's habits reflect its hunting instincts. They sleep for short intervals throughout most of the day to allow for nocturnal hunting forays – although there is a seasonal variation to this pattern – and their highly developed night vision is a useful adjunct to this.

Constant conflict

Our desire to keep our cat safely indoors at night denies him his feline hunting instinct. This is a conflict with which we need to come to terms. If the conclusion we reach is to keep the cat indoors away from the dangers of darkness, we then need to understand that for the cat, night is not a time for sleeping but for alertness and activity, and that to fulfil his basic predatory urges, we need to re-enact the preying, hunting game through play. While domestication has perhaps rendered the domestic cat less predatory by nature, and this is best seen in the selectively "bred for temperament" pedigree, beneath it all we still have a trained killer in our homes!

Food facts

Behavior such as pouncing, capturing and killing prey is practised from kittenhood. As adults, the number of caught and killed prey far outweighs the number of prey actually eaten. Birds, although often caught and killed by cats, are in fact rather inedible prey, since the feathers tend to get in the way! Hungry cats kill and eat more small prey, while mother cats make the best mousers. Preferred prey throughout the domestic cat kingdom includes rabbits, frogs, ground-nesting birds, voles, rats, spiders and other insects. Mice contain all the nutrients necessary to sustain a cat, though the presence of parasites makes mouse pie alone not a healthy option!

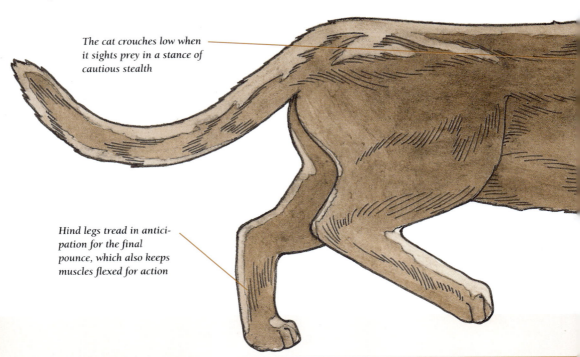

The cat crouches low when it sights prey in a stance of cautious stealth

Hind legs tread in anticipation for the final pounce, which also keeps muscles flexed for action

Play

Much of the kitten or cat's play emulates the predatory nature of its feline nature. Play is essential to enable it to re-enact the role central to its being and the one that nature intended for it. Meanwhile, playing with your kitten or cat considerably enhances the bond between you.

Boredom

A cat without anything to divert its attention will soon become very bored, especially those which are curious and lively by nature. The Oriental breeds are the likeliest candidates in the boredom stakes and can become frustrated and destructive if deprived of interaction with people, other animals and things to do.

Two's company

Two kittens together will play with each other. Take both from the same litter, or at least at the same time, and no behavioral problems should result. If spaying and neutering is carried out before their hormones start to complicate things, all should be well. For the household away at work all day, two cats would curl up together and keep each other company during those lonely hours. They will also practice their feline skills and play-fight, pounce and lie in wait for each other behind the sofa. Think it through carefully, though, before you decide to introduce two new kittens to your family.

Sleep

Cats can spend up to 60% of their days sleeping. Sleep is controlled by hormones and is induced by the chemical melatonin released in the brain. When a cat dozes off to sleep, it starts off with a period of light sleep followed by a deep sleep for a shorter period of time. On entering the deep-sleep phase, the pattern of its brainwaves changes to one resembling a wakeful state. During this time, rapid eye movement (REM) takes place and the cat can be seen to fidget and twitch during this stage. This is the time when dreaming takes place.

Cat-napping

Cat-naps, short periods of light sleep, are extremely beneficial in that they can instantly restore vitality and are remarkable fresheners when necessary. Cats can appear to be asleep with one eye open when in fact they are simply resting. The nose will be covered by the tail and to the casual observer he or she appears to be asleep. This is a device which allows it to rest and at the same time to be aware of what is happening in the vicinity!

Ears are pricked and set forward

The jaws are ideally structured to grasp small prey at the back of the neck – the teeth are inserted between the vertebrae and sever the spinal cord

Body Language

Demanding attention

Like naughty children, some cats will always demand your attention. They can find quite devious and cunning ways of doing this, such as stropping your best armchair when you are sitting in it with short, sharp bursts of scratching so you know it is not an attempt to shed claw skins but a ploy to attract your attention. It is almost impossible to break this habit and you probably have only yourself to blame for it. At some stage, you must have made a practice of giving him what he asked for when he did things which he knew annoyed you or made you give in to him.

• Ignore your cat's demands. Avoid eye contact or he will sense your annoyance – a sign that he has elicited some emotion from you, at least!

• Talk to someone else in the room while still ignoring his attention-seeking behavior.

• Leave him to it and walk out of the room after giving him your best unforgiving look.

Vocalisation

Crying, howling or screeching is the worst (or best) way possible to grab attention. If you live in the middle of nowhere with no near neighbors, confine him out of doors in a cat-house. A water pistol may distract him.

Timidity

This type of cat has had one or more fearful earlier experiences

• *If the bullying cat starts to intimidate other cats in the house-hold, you are heading for serious problems. If counselling does not work, re-homing will. Someone may be willing to take him on, or better still, the sudden change of envi-ronment could make him change his tune!*

• *Nothing is more certain to have the neighbours calling for their lawyers than a shrieking cat. You cannot de-voice him, but you could re-home him. Consult an animal behaviourist as soon as possible.*

• *Your attention-grabbing cat is a big bully. He uses forceful methods to get his own way. Best not give in to him any longer. If you can stand the pace, he could give up before you do!*

• *The flattened ears offer less of a target to the aggressor, but they can also indicate the submissive, conciliatory pose. The typical defensive posture includes a "shrinking" effect – an attempt to make the body look smaller and less threatening.*

• *Widened eyes and dilated pupils indicate fear, making the eyes appear almost black. This improves peripheral vision – useful when an attack is anticipated.*

• *A cornered or fearful cat crouches with head drawn back and ears flattened. The fur along the back and tail is erect, and the tail could be held tight to the body in a defensive gesture.*

The anxious cat

– maybe from a larger, bullying cat. Perhaps it was mistreated by its former owners. It needs all the confidence and security it can get and is best as an only cat, so that specific attention can be paid to it – not too much, otherwise it may start behaving "naughtily."

Providing refuge

If you already have domestic pets, in particular a boisterous dog in the house, then maybe the timid cat or kitten will need to live around them. Provide a high-sided cardboard box, or a completely closed one to afford greater security but with a small door cut in the side, away from other animals. Also, putting the timid cat into a transparent carrier for short periods so that it can observe the activity around but not be touched by it could gradually condition it to the outside world. Certain homeopathic or Bach flower remedies will help to boost the cat's confidence. Consult your alternative therapies vet for professional advice.

Anxiety

If this is a real problem for the cat concerned, for its own sake the very anxious cat will need medication. There could be a medical reason, either physical or mental, for this state, so consult your vet about it.

• Discover the reason for your cat's anxiety as soon as possible.

• Homeopathic remedies could help in serious cases of anxiety.
• It is in the best interests of the cat to remove the cause of its anguish as soon as possible – be it another animal or illness.

Reassurance

To know that you are there and that you care is a great help to the anxious cat. Keep calm and reassuring at all times and understand that anxious cats can sometimes be aggressive, so even if he or she turns on you occasionally, stay calm and forgiving. Periods left alone in its basket with a warm hot water bottle wrapped in a blanket will be a great comfort. Keep small children or other pets away from the cat until it has recovered.

CHAPTER 4

Health Care

A healthy cat is not only a happy cat but a fit one, too, so to maintain the general good health of your cat, a sensible health-care regime is essential.

To ensure that your cat has a nutritious diet and adequate exercise to promote strong muscles and healthy circulation is just one part of good pet-care management. Taking care that its relationships with you, your family and other domestic pets are balanced, happy and outgoing will also engender the mental well-being of your feline friend.

One of the responsibilities of cat-ownership is to ensure that regular veterinary attention is available and that vaccinations and boosters are up to date. Health insurance to fall back on should your cat need expensive veterinary care is also an investment and part of the good management plan.

All these matters, including signs of sickness, different methods of treating ailments, alternative remedial treatment at home and more, are outlined in the following pages.

You and Your Vet

Register with a vet

If you have just bought your kitten, make sure you register and present your new friend to your preferred vet as soon as possible for a general check-up. This goes for an adult cat, too. Perhaps you have just acquired one from a rescue shelter? Even though cats at most rescue centres are generally under the care of a veterinarian, you will need to introduce your new friend to a vet near you.

Your vet and you

• Should the need arise, your vet will refer your cat to a feline behavioral clinic.

• The vet will advise on procedure if you are intending to emigrate and take your pet with you.

• Your vet will probably sell specialised feline diet foods, flea products and accessories, such as leads, harnesses and toys.

• When the time comes, your vet will know of pet crematoriums and remembrance gardens in your area and will advise on procedure.

• Veterinary surgeries usually have noticeboards displaying pet animals and accessories for sale.

• The vet's noticeboard is a good place to pin-up a "lost" notice, with a photograph, should your cat go missing.

Conventional or complementary?

There are two directions in which you may go in search of regular veterinary treatment for

Pawnote:

A practitioner of either method should be informed of medication that your cat is currently taking (if any) if further treatment is being sought.

your cat – "conventional" veterinary medicine or "alternative," complementary or natural treatments and therapies. This last embraces homeopathy and herbal remedies, and also takes in crystal healing, massage, acupuncture and spiritual healing. The expert natural therapies vet studies mainstream veterinary medicine in the first instance, becoming a fully qualified veterinarian in the conventional sense, then he or she goes on to study and qualify in the field of complementary veterinary medicine.

These two methods of animal healing should, ideally, work hand in hand, since the one discipline can complement the other, but in terms of professional etiquette and the welfare of your cat, and since a mixed brew of types of medicine can be dangerous, a sensible and clear-cut decision in your choice of treatment needs to be made.

Health-care services

Veterinary centre: A fairly large establishment including the vet (the clinic owner) and one or more associate vets. There is also usually a receptionist, head veterinary nurse, a veterinary nurse and perhaps a trainee veterinary

nurse, plus an animal-care assistant who assists generally with the care of hospitalized or difficult animals and other duties. A centre manager organizes the overall smooth running of the establishment.

• Benefits: modern up-to-date equipment usually available, for instance, advanced operating equipment and on-site laboratory facilities.

Veterinary practice: A smaller establishment consisting of two or three associate partners, a receptionist, a senior veterinary nurse and a junior or trainee. It offers a small and friendly atmosphere. Equipment and treatment are as modern and up-to-date as available revenue allows. Certain blood and other tests may have to be sent to specialised centres, such as university veterinary laboratories, to be analysed.

• Benefits: friendly, personal service – probably less formal approach to client-practitioner relations; expert, often much-needed advice given over the telephone.

Availability

Nearly all veterinary services are on call for emergencies at all times. If your own vet is not on the rota when you call, one of the practice's other vets, or a locum, will be a competent stand-in. Those not providing a round-the-clock emergency service should make alternative arrangements for their clients in a case of emergency. Depending

on the country or circumstances concerned, a flying veterinary service is sometimes available to treat patients in otherwise unreachable areas.

Holding your cat for examination

It may sometimes be necessary for you to assist your vet by holding your cat still and providing reassurance if he or she is feeling anxious. For instance, if your vet is examining the cat's mouth, you will need to hold on to kitty's hindquarters. This entails a fairly firm positioning of both your hands either side of the hindquarters with forelegs steadied by two fingers. If your cat becomes really frantic, wrap him firmly in a towel and proceed with ministrations. If the vet is dealing with your cat's rear end, restrain front legs with one hand and hold up the cat's head with your other hand – at the same time restraining the jaws but keeping the nose free.

Health insurance

While not every owner sees this as a sensible step to take, insurance undoubtedly takes the worry out of unexpected veterinary bills. For example, accidents and boarding cattery fees if you are ill, cancellation of holiday costs if your cat suddenly falls ill just as you are about to depart or if your cat goes missing or worse. So why take the risk?

The breeder who exhibits and travels to shows is not often without "breeders' cover," insuring against stud and queen sickness, accident, theft, loss or death, as well as breakdown while travelling to a show by car, etc. New policies for pet owners are emerging every day. Keep in touch, consult your vet or get quotes from a wide range of insurance companies and assess cover offered and relevant costs of each.

Encompass your cat's hindquarters with both hands, to restrain any defensive reaction from the strong back legs

Part the first two fingers of each hand to also restrain the forelegs

Vaccinations

All cats coming into contact with other cats – and even if they do not – need to be vaccinated against a variety of feline diseases. The kitten or cat without such protection is severely at risk from infection.

A kitten should first be vaccinated against major diseases prevalent in your area or country between eight to ten weeks, when mother's milk no longer cancels out antibodies introduced into her kitten's system. A second dose should be given at 12 weeks. In the pedigree kitten, the breeder will be responsible for carrying out the initial two stages of vaccination. The kitten should then not be allowed out of doors or to come in contact with other cats, since immunity is not complete until two weeks after the final dose. When the kitten reaches cathood, a booster will be required at 15 months. Further boosters will be required at later stages. All details of vaccinations will be recorded on your cat's vaccination card.

Consult your vet for information regarding your cat, its and your circumstances and subsequent necessity for vaccination against these diseases. The following are major feline diseases against which it is recommended that your cat is vaccinated.

Feline panleucopenia (viral enteritis)

Highly infectious, causing the often fatal gastroenteritis and frequently seen in the kitten, although any cat coming into

contact with another infected cat or infected object can fall victim. The virus can remain active up to one year outside the cat's body.

Symptoms: Usually include fever, diarrhea, vomiting, lethargy; the cat will crave water but will not eat. Severe in the young kitten.

Treatment: No specific treatment available. Vaccination provides a long-lasting, high level of protection.

Feline upper respiratory disease (cat flu)

Generally caused by one of two viruses – Feline Calicivirus (FCV) or Feline Viral Rhinotracheitis (FVR), also known as feline herpesvirus (FHV). Infection occurs through direct contact with other cat(s) suffering from the disease and is commonly found in colonies of cats, either feral or breeding groups, or in boarding catteries.

Symptoms: FVR can lead to more severe symptoms but both include fever, sneezing, tongue ulcers, lack of appetite, eye and nasal discharges. Depression follows.

Treatment: Vaccination means that the severity of the disease is significantly reduced. Antibiotics are used to combat general bacterial infection.

Feline chlamydial infection

Mainly found in kittens and/or in large colonies of cats, it is the common cause of conjunctivitis and could be an added compli-

cation of cat flu. Infection caused by direct contact with a cat that is currently suffering or has recovered from but is still "shedding" the disease.

Symptoms: Weeping eyes; reddened, swelling, inflamed and painful conjunctiva – the membrane around the eye. There could be a nasal discharge and some sneezing. Eating is often not affected.

Treatment: Certain antibiotics are effective in controlling the infection. Vaccination is available but is generally given to kittens which are exposed to cats which have, or which recently have had, the infection.

Feline Leukaemia Virus Infection (FeLV)

Belonging to the group of viruses known as "retroviruses," FeLV was a scourge among cats in the late 1970s and onwards. Highly infectious, this is an immunodeficiency-type virus similar in effect to the human HIV, but is in no way "cat AIDS." Passed on via bod fluids, i.e. saliva, blood, milk, mucous and faeces of (permanently) infected cats. Fighting cats are at risk due to bites and other incisions. Cats may recover but will always carry the disease. Kittens can be infected via the placenta or by an infected mother's milk.

Symptoms: Initial infection during incubation may go unnoticed; the cat may be "off color." As the immune system becomes less efficient, various other infections and diseases may be evident. Weight loss; anaemia;

gum disease; mouth ulcers; diarrhea and vomiting are general outward symptoms of the lowered immune system. Cats can seem to be active while the virus is being shed to other vulnerable cats. Cats remain permanently infected.

Treatment: Currently, no drugs are available to specifically treat FeLV. Secondary problems may be treated individually. Most infected cats die within $3^{1}/_{2}$ years of being infected. If your household contains infected cat(s), the remainder should be tested for FeLV. Positive and negative cats should each be sectioned off in two separate colonies; disinfection of implements and bedding should be totally scrupulous, and owners should seriously consider putting tested positive cats to sleep. Vaccination can be given, but this only makes sense with tested negative cats.

Feline Immunodeficiency Virus (FIV)

Infection by this virus results in immunosuppression, which means an inability to combat infection and disease. One of the group of retroviruses of which FeLV (above) is one. Suspect cats are blood-tested to discover negative or positive status. FIV is similar to HIV, the virus responsible for human AIDS.

Symptoms: The cat may be "off color" and will suffer various recurring infections due to its immune-suppressive state. Transferred via cat fights, bites and transmission of blood, saliva, etc. Prognosis is as for FeLV infected cats (see page 70).

Treatment: No drugs are specifically available to treat FIV positive cats. Subsidiary conditions may be treated with antibiotics. Consult your vet for an update on available treatments.

Feline coronavirus infection (Feline Infectious Peritonitis or FIP)

Transmitted via saliva or faeces of infected cats, this is a slowly progressive and fatal disease and longevity is determined by the state of the immune system. There are two types of this virus – "wet" FIP and "dry" FIP. Differ-entiation from leukaemia/ lymphosarcoma and toxoplasmosis has to be defined.

Symptoms: "Wet" FIP: fever, depression, lack of appetite, weight loss leading to emaciation and distension of the abdomen owing to exudate (fluid). "Dry" FIP is more difficult to diagnose and may involve liver, kidney, eye and brain disease. Granulomas in the kidney may also be found.

Treatment: No drugs are specifically available to treat FIP and most cats die as a result of having it. Consult your vet for an update on available treatments.

Signs of Ill Health

Common problems

As custodians of our cat's health and well-being, we need to be aware of what may or may not get out of balance with the proper functioning of our cat's bodies. Here are some of the health hazards which may affect a cat at each stage of his or her life.

Pawnote:

For all of these suspected conditions (right), consult your veterinarian to obtain an accurate diagnosis and subsequent treatment

Kittens (birth to nine months old)

There are three phases to kittenhood: neonatal, the first fortnight of its life when the mother is relied upon solely for all its needs; socialization, the third or fourth week, when the kitten becomes receptive to its environment, people and other animals; and juvenile, at around two months old, when the kitten recognizes and becomes attached to its human mother and relates to her or him in a positive way.

Neonatal: Possible health hazards could be genetically inherited defects, i.e. flat-chestedness, cleft palate, etc.; following birth, respiratory problems, intestines appearing outside the body, mother-related difficulties, i.e. poor mothering, the kitten's inability to suck milk, hypother-

Owing to the somewhat secretive nature of the cat that is unwell, it may be difficult to spot the onset of illness in your own pet feline. However, daily checking of teeth and gums, eyes, monitoring food and water intake and evidence of mites, fleas and worms may reveal early signs. Here are symptoms which could indicate that something is wrong:

Symptoms	Degrees of/and likely causes
* Bad breath and drooling	Mouth infection or disease
* Coughing and/or gagging	Allergy; bronchitis; chest infection
* Shaking head and scratching ears	Ear mites and/or infection
* Breathing difficulties	Chest and upper respiratory tract disease
* Vomiting	Hairballs; diet or other causes
* Loss of appetite	Temporary or lasting over 2 days
* Loss of weight	Steady decline
* Urinary problems	Straining; decreased/increased urine
* Behavioral changes	See vet for diagnosis/referral
* Excess licking	Parasites or allergies
* Sneezing/nasal discharge	Allergy or viral infection
* Watering/inflamed eyes	Conjunctivitis or viral infection
* Dragging posterior on the floor	Worm infestation
* Diarrhea or constipation	Diet-induced; infection or parasites
* Loss of balance	Stroke; middle-ear infection; blood loss

mia. Also "fading" kitten syndrome and damaged limbs (hanging in an awkward way) due to being lain on by its mother.
Socialization: General weakness and "fading" kitten syndrome. Diseases inherited in the womb or through infected

mother's milk, such as cat flu, chlamydia etc. Still be aware of the damaged limb possibility.
Juvenile: Feline panleucopenia (viral enteritis), severe in kittens and often fatal. Kittens at this stage are vulnerable to most of the feline infectious diseases.

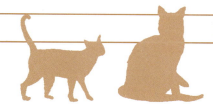

From juvenile to 9 months: Any of the feline infectious diseases and accidents occurring during normal kitten activities.

Adults
(nine months to 9 years)

Even the well-nourished (but un-vaccinated) cat is still extremely vulnerable to all the feline infectious diseases. Spayed or neutered cats stand slightly less chance due to their probably decreased contact with other cats outdoors. "Stud tail," affecting both sexes, neutered or not, is an over-production of sebum causing soreness, irritability and hair loss under the tail. Road traffic accidents, loss of limbs, injury due to cat-fights, etc. are almost always preventable hazards. Important conditions to be aware of are diabetes, tumours/cancer, kidney and bladder problems. Minor conditions include abscesses, dermatitis, eczema and skin allergies.

Old age
(from age 10 onwards)

Elderly felines may become disorientated, incontinent and subject to irrational behavior, such as periods of activity alternating with lethargy. Sleep patterns will change to give longer periods of deep sleep, periods of fitful, twitching (REM) sleep and longer periods of cat-napping. A lowered immune system will mean increased vulnerability to infection. Heart problems are not uncommon with the older cat; years of youthful activity will begin to tell on an increasingly less effective circulatory system. Lungs and blood pressure will need to be regularly checked by your vet. Hearing, eyesight and reflex actions will begin to deteriorate and slow down. Obesity is a problem with the older, less active cat; also an over-active thyroid, kidney and urinary tract disorders and disease. Gum disease and loss of teeth may affect eating habits.

Drooling and bad breath can indicate mouth disease – gingivitis, mouth ulcers and/or decaying teeth

Weight loss can be age-related; this may or may not be a natural trend in your cat's eating habits – consult your vet

Listlessness, increased lassitude and loss of appetite could indicate thyroid problems

Visible "hawes" (third eyelid stretching from the inside of the eye across the eyeball) indicates he or she is unwell

Checking for Problems

If your cat is sick

Before you call out your vet or discuss the problems you are experiencing with your cat, it is as well to do some checking out first, so that at least you can clearly describe to your vet the symptoms of your cat's condition. This will be helpful and save time in an emergency.

Signs of illness in your cat could be: fever (high temperature); lassitude; drifting in and out of sleep; loss of appetite; restlessness; excessive drinking or not drinking at all; abdominal swelling; excessive urination, or straining with little urination; diarrhoea or constipation; vomiting.

Take your cat's temperature

1. The healthy cat's temperature is normally around 38.5°C (101.3°F). To take your cat's temperature properly, you will need someone to restrain the cat by holding its scruff firmly and restraining the two front legs.
2. Shake and set the thermometer and cover the end with a lubricant jelly. Hold up the cat's tail with your left hand and insert the thermometer into the anal ring, twisting gently to do this with ease. Ensure that the tip of the thermometer is well into the cat's anus.
3. Carefully holding the thermometer in place, leave it there for 40-60 seconds, or as directed on the instruction leaflet
4. Remove and wipe it clean with a dampened swab, then read the temperature and record this, along with the time and date.

Take your cat's pulse

The pulse rate of a healthy cat at rest is around 110–140 beats per minute. Breathing rate is between 24 and 42 breaths per minute.

1. Find the pulse which is on the inner thigh, close to the groin.
2. With the first two fingers of your right hand, check the pulse for a full minute.

Monitor fluid intake

Measure out bottled mineral water into the cat's drinking bowl. Mark the level poured and check the amount consumed over a period of 12 hours.

Monitor food intake

1. Weigh and measure out canned or other food which your cat would normally eat. Monitor how much, if any, has been consumed over a 12-hour period.
2. If no food has been eaten for 36 hours, ensure water at least is taken. This may have to be given by pipette or syringe inserted through the soft side of the mouth and behind the canine teeth. Gently stroke the throat to help the water go down. To prevent choking, wait for your cat to swallow before offering more. On completion of your findings, make detailed notes and contact your vet.

Check weight

You should, in any case, regularly weigh your cat on flat kitchen scales to monitor any changes, but now that he or she is off-color, it is a good time to pay particular attention to weight loss or gain.

1. The best way to weigh your cat is to first weigh its carrying case, then put your cat inside and subtract the carrier's weight from the overall weight of cat and carrier.

2. Weigh your cat once every 36 hours to identify weight loss, if any. This way of monitoring your cat's weight is also useful during periods of convalescence.

Observe breathing

Notice your cat's breathing patterns. Is it noisy? Is it wheezy? Is breathing shallow or labored? Difficulty in breathing could indicate a respiratory infection or heart disease, or that he or she has sinus problems.

Assess behavior

Any change in the behavioral norm of your cat is suspect and could indicate both mental and/or physical disease. Is your cat restless or aggressive when handled? Does it show sudden alternate bouts of activity and lethargy? Are there unpredictable mood swings, fearfulness or perhaps a constant purring?

Early consultation with your vet is required for appraisal of any of the above or other symptoms. Delay could be fatal.

Emergency first-aid kit

Sometimes, remedial measures need to be taken, if only to prevent an accident becoming an emergency. Why not create your own first-aid kit so that you can cope with basic medical requirements? Here are some essential items to include in your kit:

- A sheet of silver foil or bubble wrap, to preserve body heat and prevent a drop in body temperature following severe shock
- Cotton wool
- Moist face wipes and swabs or cotton buds
- Disposable gloves
- Large towel
- Veterinary antiseptic (none containing phenol) or small bottle of tea tree essential oil (dilute as directed)
- Salt, for preparing a saline solution for bathing wounds
- Cotton bandage and wide elastic bandage, plus adhesive tape to tape bandage into position
- Sterile dressings
- Gauze impregnated with lanolin
- Gauze pads for staunching blood
- Long, round-ended scissors
- Tweezers
- Thermometer
- Magnifying glass
- Flashlight and spare batteries

- Arnica ointment to help prevent or minimize bruising; this also helps to stop bleeding and heal damaged tissue
- Calendula (lotion or ointment) – apply directly to a wound to promote healing
- Bach Flower's Rescue Remedy, given by mouth in single drops (1 drop every 5 minutes) is helpful for shock resulting from injury; also helpful in calming the distressed cat
- Lavender oil is soothing if massaged around an insect bite or sting (not for use with open wounds)
- Two copies of a first-aid handbook describing artificial respiration (mouth to mouth) and resuscitation procedure – one copy for the first-aid kit, the other for serious reading in your spare time, to prepare you for tackling emergencies

Eye Problems

Signs and symptoms

Your cat's eyes indicate and reflect its current state of physical and often mental health. Allergies, foreign bodies, infection and feline viral disease can all cause or be contributing factors to eye conditions or disease. Signs which could indicate problems include:

- Rubbing or pawing at an irritated eye
- Reddened, weeping (discharging) eye(s)
- Swollen membranes surrounding the eye
- Partly closed, infected (reddened) eyelids
- Blinking
- Evading bright light

Presence of both third eyelids indicates problems with each eye.

Conjunctivitis

Caused by inflammation of the conjunctival membranes, this is one of the most common eye problems. It can be caused by an organism known as *Chlamydia psittaci* (see page 70) and is a symptom of specific feline viral infection, i.e. feline upper respiratory disease or cat flu. Veterinary treatment will include antibiotics as appropriate.

Cataracts

An eye condition in which coagulation of the plasma of cells in the lens with subsequent loss of transparency occurs; a bluish, cloudy appearance results and vision becomes blurred. This can be a congenital condition or one associated with the diabetic or elderly cat. If one eye only is affected, surgery is not always necessary but can be used to restore vision to one eye when both are affected.

Keratitis

An inflammation of the cornea, keratitis may result from conjunctivitis or following injury to or infection of the cornea itself. A whitish ring appears around the cornea and should this progress, opacity becomes obvious. Other corneal disorders include oedema and ulceration. Early signs are watering of the eye and sensitivity. Urgent veterinary treatment is essential.

Glaucoma

This is a serious condition where the tension of fluid content of the eyeball is greatly in excess of the normal. Swelling and bulging of one or both eyes results and blindness can follow. Urgent treatment is essential at early recognition of symptoms.

Epiphora

This occurs when normal drainage of tears is impeded and tears overflow onto the face. It can be an inherited factor or inherent to a particular breed, i.e. the Persian Longhair. Dark tear-staining to the facial fur results and can be difficult to remove. Consult your vet, who may flush the tear ducts. Surgery is rarely attempted.

Third eyelids

The nictitating membrane or "third eyelid" tissue is sometimes seen to protrude across the eyeball. This is an automatic self-protective response and a sign that a) your cat is generally unwell b) has viral infection or c) the eyeball itself has been injured.

This condition may be permanent if as a kitten your cat suffered from cat flu or another virus infection. Those with this problem will always be vulnerable to eye injury or infection. Consult your vet in all instances of the above.

Ear Problems

Signs and symptoms

The cat's sense of balance and hearing are controlled by the ear, a sensitive organ which is also a communications device, a sound receiver and a ventilating system for the inner canals. Symptoms which could indicate problems are:
- Smelly deposits
- Scratching, head-shaking and rubbing the face on the ground
- Inability to respond to sound
- Reddened ear hole
- Resistance to handling or fondling around the ear
- Infected ear flap

Otitis externa

Inflammation of the external ear canal is a very common complaint in cats and can be symptomatic of many conditions. Basically, the problem is caused by excess scratching for various reasons – parasitic ear mites (see page 83), infection, a foreign body, fungus or bacteria. Consult your vet immediately if you notice your cat scratching its ear(s).

Mange

Certain types of mange can begin on the pinna (part of the external ear). Auricular or otodectic mange involves the presence of mites (*otodectes cyanotis*). Consult your vet at the first sign of symptoms.

Foreign bodies

These could be hay seeds, sand, pieces of glass, wood or any item small enough to lodge in the cat's ear canal. Scratching, irritation and infection could follow if veterinary advice is not sought.

Deafness

Partial or complete, temporary or permanent deafness can be due to middle-ear infection, head injury, old age or as a result of the ear canal becoming blocked with wax. Deafness in white cats with blue eyes is an inherited factor and breeding of these cats is discouraged in the pedigree world. For correct diagnosis and to find out if the condition is treatable or irreversible, consult your vet immediately.

Middle-ear infection

This is always dangerous since it could lead to loss of hearing and balance and also meningitis (inflammation affecting the brain and/or spine). The cat will generally tilt its head to one side. Consult your vet immediately to avoid delay in treatment.

Wounds

Injuries caused by fighting or accident require urgent attention to prevent infection. Haematomas (blood blisters) can cause irritation when scratched; your vet can drain these of fluid and provide a support to keep the shape and prevent collapse.

Sunburn

An over-exposure to ultra-violet light (UVB) or sunlight can cause burning and a cancerous state if prevention is not carried out and treatment is delayed (see pages 86 and 125 for more information).

Frostbite

Ears, paws and tail can be affected by low temperatures and resulting hypothermia. If treatment is delayed, necrosis can set in and essential amputation of ear tips result.

Mouth Problems

Signs and symptoms

Designed to assist the predating cat, teeth, gums and tongue all play an important role and problems occur when damage or disease prevents the normal usage of the mouth. Symptoms are:

- Lack of appetite
- Bad breath
- Inflamed gum edges
- Receding gums
- Yellow/brown deposits on the teeth at gum margin
- Drooling and pawing at the mouth

Gum disease (Gingivitis)

Gingivitis is associated with a build-up of tartar or calculus which forms on the teeth at the gum margin. Consult your vet at the first sign of inflamed gums.
• A regular mouth-care regime using a small soft toothbrush and pet toothpaste would prevent this problem.

Mouth infection

This term covers a variety of problems. Gingivitis-stomatitis is one where not only gums but the whole mouth lining becomes inflamed. This may be a sudden acute attack or a long-term condition. Feline Immunodeficiency Virus (FIV) and kidney problems could be the reason for this type of infection. Mouth ulcers can also be attributed to this cause. Consult your vet at an early stage for diagnosis and treatment.

Rodent ulcers

Probably caused by over-licking (lick granuloma), a rodent ulcer appears as a raised sore or swelling, usually on the upper lip. Veterinary treatment is essential and should be completed or the condition will recur.

Cleft palate

This condition is an inherited defect of the mouth, and can occur as a result of in-breeding. Rarer reasons for the occurrence of the condition include an iodine deficiency in the pregnant queen. It consists of a gap in the structures forming the palate. There are varying degrees in the severity of the condition, but generally kittens born with a cleft palate cannot suckle properly and milk can be seen coming from the nostrils. In some cases, surgery can repair the palate.

Internal parasites

Roundworm

The commonest form of intestinal infestation is *toxocara cati*. The adult worm can be up to 15 cm (6 in) in length. Infestation in the kitten can occur via infected mother's milk, the litter tray and by ingestion while grooming. Also caused by eating infected prey, i.e. birds, rodents or rabbits.
Signs: Probably none in the early stages. Later, if undetected infestation increases, there could be diarrhea, swollen abdomen, general lassitude and poor coat condition. Worms passed in the feces are often first detected in the litter tray.
Treatment: Consult your vet.
Prevention: Regular doses of worming treatment, before mating in the queen and routinely 3 or 4 times a year for a hunting cat allowed to roam.

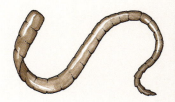

Tapeworm

The most common tapeworm to infest cats is *dipylidium caninum*, which affects mainly the adult cat. Tapeworms are

Internal Parasites

flat, segmented, white in colour and can grow up to 30 cm (12 in) in length. Segments of adult tapeworm are shed from the cat's anus.

Signs: White segments appearing around the cat's anus, a cat's intensive grooming to its bottom, diarrhea, general lassitude and poor coat condition.

Treatment: Consult your vet.

Prevention: Regular worming two or three times a year plus strict flea control of both cat and environment.

Hookworm

The blood-sucking hookworm, *ancylostoma tubaeforme,* is the more commonly seen species in cats. Living in the small intestine, the mature female hookworm lays 10,000-30,000 eggs per day. It is from 5-12 mm ($\frac{1}{4}$-$\frac{1}{2}$ in) in length and grey-white in color, unless infused with blood. Infective larvae can be swallowed or penetrate the skin of feet or stomach.

Signs: Diarrhea and weight loss.

Treatment: Consult your vet.

Prevention: Strict and constant hygiene measures.

Pawnote:

Most worm infestations are transmissible to humans. Cats should be wormed on a regular basis and strict hygiene should be observed at all times. Cats should not be allowed to sit on kitchen benches and dining tables nor be kissed or have facial contact with humans. Wash hands thoroughly (especially children) after handling your cat and before eating or handling food.

Heartworm

A common disease in dogs but quite rare in cats. Occurring in tropical or subtropical areas. The worm, *dirofilaria immitis,* lives in the right ventricle of the heart and the pulmonary artery and can vary from 10-25 cm (4-10 in) in length. Larvae are released into the bloodstream and certain types of mosquitoes, having ingested the blood, can release the larvae into the bloodstream of another animal.

Signs: Lethargy, chronic cough, excessive thirst, anaemia and labored breathing.

Treatment: Diagnosed by blood tests. An arsenical compound injected intravenously kills the heartworm, followed by drugs to kill the larvae.

Prevention: Tablets are available to prevent heartworm.

Lungworms

Found in the lungs of infected cats and inhabiting the terminal bronchioles and smaller branches of the pulmonary artery. The predating cat may become infected by birds, snails, slugs or rodents carrying the larvae.

Signs: Few, but there could be a persistent, dry cough.

Treatment: Consult your vet.

Prevention: None unless the hunting cat is restricted to an indoor lifestyle.

Threadworm and whipworm

These are small, thin worms which live in the cat's gut and cause fewer problems than the other worms mentioned here. They are found in parts of Australia and the US.

Signs: Infestation rarely causes illness, but the cat could suffer from diarrhea.

Treatment: Consult your vet.

Prevention: None except routine examination of the litter tray for evidence and constant observation of strict hygiene measures.

Digestive Problems

Signs and symptoms

The digestive system breaks down food from its varied ingredients of protein, carbohydrates, fats, etc. into a manageable mix of molecules, which are then absorbed into the bloodstream through the small intestinal wall. Signs of problems are:

- Sickness/vomiting
- Diarrhea/constipation
- Refusal to eat
- Weight loss
- Excessive thirst
- Dietary sensitivity

Vomiting

Cats vomit after eating grass (sometimes a method to rid the gut of parasites). They can also regurgitate hairballs (hair ingested while grooming, especially in the longhair). Projectile vomiting a short period after eating food indicates a blockage; sour, yellow vomit can mean gastric problems and vomit containing whole, undigested food could indicate an intolerance to that particular food.

Cats are discriminatory in their eating habits. They will instinctively ignore food unacceptable to them, will probably not touch contaminated food and do not eat just for the sake of eating. Observe your cat's vomiting pattern and consult your vet if it continues for more than 24 hours.

Diarrhoea

Can be caused by stress, infection, worm infestation, poisoning, Feline Infectious Enteritis (FIE), an inability to absorb food or, in the mature cat, due to the presence of tumors or cancer. Straining to evacuate faeces should not be confused with constipation. Diarrhea accompanied by vomiting and/or if blood is also present could indicate a serious problem. Consult your vet as soon as possible.

Constipation

The cat will normally evacuate faeces at least once each day. Less than this could indicate that dietary content needs to be re-assessed, that there could be an intestinal blockage or that simply your cat requires a cat laxative or a dose of liquid paraffin (by mouth). If a bowel movement has not occurred for 48 hours, consult a vet immediately.

Feline Infectious Enteritis (FIE)

Largely seen in the kitten, FIE or feline panleucopenia or viral enteritis (see page 70) can be a fatal disease. Persistent diarrhea and vomiting occur causing serious weight loss and careful nursing is required to prevent dehydration. FIE is extremely contagious. Vaccination will provide a high level of protection but for the kitten or cat suffering from FIE, early diagnosis and isolation from other cats is essential.

Feline Infectious Peritonitis (FIP)

Caused by a coronavirus, FIP is a slowly progressive and generally fatal disease of mainly young cats. FIP virus primarily causes infection of the abdominal cavity (see page 71). This highly contagious disease develops quickly so that death may occur before diagnosis can be made. No vaccine is available and treatment is generally ineffective.

Liver disease

The liver may be affected or damaged by viral disease, poison, cancer, lymphoma, increased thyroid hormones, Feline Infectious Peritonitis (FIP) and also by abnormalities and defects present at birth.

Symptoms: A general lassitude and jaundice, which is most clearly seen in the yellowing of the whites of the eyes.
- Vomiting and/or diarrhea
- Excessive thirst
- Reduced appetite or anorexia
- Weight loss
- Depression and lethargy
- Abdominal pain and/or swelling

Treatment: Veterinary diagnosis will be made by analysing samples of blood, urine and faeces. Severe cases may merit intensive care involving the introduction of fluid by intravenous drip and food fed by tube. Dietary control and modification will be necessary to reduce build-up of protein-processed waste in the liver.

Examining the cat for abdominal swelling

Specially formulated diets are available for felines with liver disease.

Prognosis: With dietary control and the specially formulated foods for liver-disease sufferers mentioned above, plenty of clean water to drink and regular veterinary checks, the condition can be kept under control. Liver infections and gall stones in the bile duct can be complications.

Diabetes

There are two types: *Diabetes mellitus,* hyperglycaemia or sugar diabetes and *diabetes insipidus,* known as water diabetes. *Diabetes mellitus* is the more common variety in cats and is a condition in which there is an inadequate production of insulin by the pancreas. Sugar diabetes affects the more mature cat, probably those over the age of six years. Male cats are more likely to develop the condition than the female, and neutered cats are nearly twice as likely to develop the disease than entire cats.

Symptoms: Decreased insulin levels mean blood-glucose levels are too high (glucose is lost together with water through the kidneys) causing the affected cat to pass more urine than normal.

• Excessive thirst and urination
• Change in appetite; increased or, more often, decreased
• Weight loss
• Poor coat condition
• Bowel motions are often of a putty consistency and colour
• Lethargy and depression

Treatment: Diagnosis will be confirmed by blood sugar and urine tests. Hospitalization will be necessary to stabilize the cat's blood sugar level by giving insulin injections. Following this, your vet will show you how this is done, so that you can give the daily injections at home (see page 99). The veterinarian will regularly monitor your cat's blood sugar level.

Prognosis: Providing your cat is given daily insulin injections, he or she can enjoy a relatively healthy life. Confined roaming space will allow you to take the regular urine samples required and to monitor litter trays.

Dietary sensitivity

Food hypersensitivity or allergy is a specific sensitivity to plant or animal products, usually of a protein nature. The dietary sensitivity is less common than the flea-bite hypersensitivity or the atopic – hypersensitivity to pollen, giving hay-fever like symptoms.

Symptoms:
• Itching, with self-inflicted damage as a result
• Redness
• Sometimes edema of the face, ears, vulva or extremities
• Skin weals

Treatment: When the reason for the sensitivity is not known, full veterinary examination should be carried out to discover the cause(s). Meanwhile, treatment regimes include anti-inflammatory medicines and creams to soothe the irritation and hyposensitisation techniques which aim to make the immune system less reactive to the substance(s) causing the condition.

Prognosis: Avoidance of the foods causing the hypersensitivity is the satisfactory answer to long-term control and meanwhile, careful vigilance on your behalf is necessary to monitor cat food ingredients. Consult your vet for specially prepared diets for hypersensitive cats to ensure a healthy, rash-free life.

External Parasites

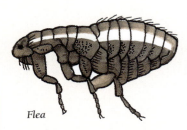

Flea

Fleas

The prolific, parasitic flea, owners vow, is an integral part of the cat's life and certainly constant vigilance is required to keep them at bay. Fleas spend most of their existence in the environment but jump onto the warm-blooded cat or dog to feed and breed. They live off dead skin debris and bite through the cat's skin with their needle-like mouthparts to suck the blood. They mate, lay hundreds of eggs which hatch out to live in the environment (your home), hitch a ride on a passing cat and the whole cycle starts again. From 10 fleas, over 250,000 can develop in only one month.

Prevention: Spray environment (your home) regularly with flea deterrents – furnishings, rugs, spaces between carpet and wall and especially around radiators.

Conventional treatment: Any of the proprietary brand flea deterrents used for the recommended period of time.

Alternative treatment: Sulphur (homeopathic); one

dose weekly as a preventive measure. Eucalyptus oil dabbed onto the tick; Pennyroyal, Fleabane and Tansy (herbal) may be sprinkled around the cat's bedding. A daily dose of half chopped clove of garlic added to food will deter fleas (herbal); also, a daily bath in vinegar (half to half water) and brewer's yeast sprinkled onto the coat or taken orally.

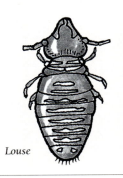

Louse

Lice

Pediculosis or infestation by lice is caused by close contact with infected cats, grooming equipment or bedding. Lice are small, wingless, flat-bodied creatures which feed on the cat's hair and skin debris. Infestation is generally in old and debilitated cats or those living in crowded, unhygienic conditions. Lice survive only a few days away from their host.

Prevention: Spray the cat's environment regularly with

proprietary brand flea deterrents (see left). Observe hygienic conditions for your cat and its surroundings. Maintain his or her good health by feeding balanced, nutritious meals.

Conventional treatment: As for fleas and ticks.

Alternative treatment: As for fleas and ticks.

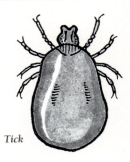

Tick

Ticks

Ticks or "sheep ticks," those found particularly on cats, are eight-legged creatures related to spiders which infest cats in the spring and autumn. They are picked up by the cat brushing against infected plants, grasses, etc. and bury their heads in the cat's skin to feed on the blood, becoming more noticeable to the naked eye after having taken a meal. Heavy infestation can cause anaemia.

Prevention: Proprietary brand flea deterrents, but to avoid infection and/or allergic reaction, care should be taken to

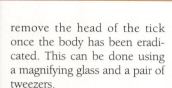

remove the head of the tick once the body has been eradicated. This can be done using a magnifying glass and a pair of tweezers.

Conventional treatment: As for fleas and lice.

Alternative treatment: As for fleas and lice.

Mites

Three parasites belong to the mites group – the Cheyletiella mite, ear mite and the harvest mite.

Ear mite

ear, scattered when the head is shaken. Infection causes irritation to the skin of the ear canal and produces a dark brown or black debris.

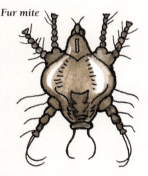

Fur mite

Harvest mite

The **Cheyletiella** (fur mite) spends its entire life on the skin of the infected cat, and is transmitted by direct contact with other infected cats. Symptoms are scaly skin flakes (dandruff), excessive scratching, head-shaking and/or hypersensitive reaction to bites causing miliary dermatitis (see page 86).

The **ear mite** (*otodectes cyanotis*) is easily transmitted by debris from the infected cat's

The **harvest mite** is prevalent during late summer and autumn and is picked up from the ground, causing parasitic infection first to feet, legs, head and ears. There is extreme irritation and sometimes hypersensitive reaction causing miliary dermatitis. Veterinary diagnosis and treatment for the above mite infestation is essential, as is aftercare, such as frequent grooming

to remove remaining debris, eggs, etc. and close inspection of the skin to detect signs of eczema/dermatitis or inflamed raised bumps which could become abscessed.

Conventional treatment: Consult your veterinarian for specific treatment following diagnosis.

Alternative treatment: Consult your veterinarian for specific treatment following diagnosis. For general mite infestation, this could include: Sulphur for the infected cat who dislikes heat; Psorinum for one who likes heat (homeopathic); Rosemary, Thyme, Tea tree or Rue, orally as directed, or as a lotion to apply to infected parts. Ear mites: the above remedies include Calendula lotion, garlic lotion or slightly warmed olive oil to clean the ears (herbal).

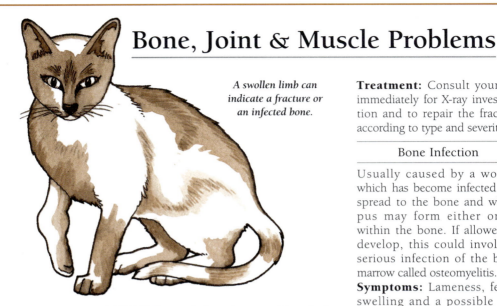

Bone, Joint & Muscle Problems

A swollen limb can indicate a fracture or an infected bone.

Signs and symptoms

The cat is naturally agile and flexible in its movements, so accidental damage to its refined skeletal structure, well-protected by a muscular covering, is quite rare. Accidents on the road, dietary insufficiencies and/or excesses, infections and bone disease such as arthritis, sadly, are not. Symptoms of bone, joint and muscle problems include:

- Fever, swelling and perhaps discharge around the affected part
- Temporary or intermittent lameness
- Noticeable physical aberration or deformity
- Limping
- Swollen legs and feet
- Signs of having been in a fight

Dislocation

Most commonly occurring after an accident of some sort or a fall; the hip is usually affected. However, any of the joints and including the jaw, although this is rare, can become dislocated.
Symptoms: An inability to put weight on a limb, an unwillingness to play and pain when touched in the injured area.
Treatment: Urgent veterinary treatment is essential. The vet will anaesthetise the cat and replace the joint in its socket.

Bone fractures

A simple or closed fracture is where the bone does not break through the skin, whereas a compound fracture has an open wound which leads down to the bone damage. Most fractures are suffered in road traffic accidents, where a direct injury to the limb or limbs is incurred. Gunshot wounds or being kicked or trodden on can also be the cause of fractures.
Symptoms: Swelling of the affected limb(s) and obvious pain when touched (simple fracture); skin wounds and broken bone showing through (compound fracture).

Treatment: Consult your vet immediately for X-ray investigation and to repair the fracture according to type and severity.

Bone Infection

Usually caused by a wound which has become infected and spread to the bone and where pus may form either on or within the bone. If allowed to develop, this could involve a serious infection of the bone marrow called osteomyelitis.
Symptoms: Lameness, fever, swelling and a possible discharge from the affected part.
Treatment: Urgent veterinary treatment is essential. Antibiotics will be used to treat the infection. If serious infection has been allowed to develop, amputation of the limb (or tail) may be advisable.

Vitamin excess (hypervitaminosis)

This can result in serious disease, for instance in cats fed mainly on liver or heart. If this food is fed, one or two meals per week should be the maximum. An excess of liver (vitamin A) can cause deformities of the spine and a diet of exclusively heart meat can cause paralysis within a matter of weeks. Too much vitamin D is also harmful. An exclusive diet of all-muscle meat such as minced beef can produce skeletal deformities.
Symptoms: As above.
Treatment: Immediate dietary control. Do not give vitamin supplements unless recommended by your vet.

Sprains

Minor injuries such as sprains can occur when a muscle tendon or ligament is strained in perhaps an awkward fall or an ill-judged leap from a height.
Symptoms: Swelling and temporary lameness.
Treatment: Under veterinary supervision, sprains may be treated at home.

Arthritis

Commonly referred to as "joint inflammation," arthritis often follows bone infection. Osteoarthritis is concerned with the growth of new bone around a joint and deterioration of the smooth cartilage that covers and protects the end of the bones within the joint. Traumatic arthritis sprain may be caused by a sudden injury to the joint, including tearing or stretching of the soft tissue and ligaments within or surrounding the joint.
Symptoms: Traumatic arthritis – swollen and/or painful joints, limping and pain when handled. Osteoarthritis – stiffness and limping, particularly following rest. Severity of symptoms may fluctuate according to cold/damp or fine/warm weather. New bone growth around joints.
Treatment: Consult your vet immediately for diagnosis and to determine affected joints. A short course of anti-inflammatory drugs may be prescribed to relieve the condition. Further treatment will depend on the severity of the condition.

Allergies

Apart from allergic reactions that have an effect on the respiratory system (see page 89), cats can suffer from the following:

Flea-bite hypersensitivity

An allergy to flea-bites is one of the most common of the feline skin conditions, caused by an immune reaction to the saliva injected into the cat's body as it sucks the blood. Causing a local allergic reaction, this irritates the cat which then scratches and bites to obtain temporary relief. Aggravation to the skin, which becomes inflamed and causes more irritation, follows.
Symptoms: Localized areas of red, inflamed skin with abrasions which eventually become encrusted scabs.
Treatment: Intensive regime of flea control (see page 82). If the attacks are severe, short-term use of anti-inflammatory drugs or the use of alternative methods to deter fleas (see page 82). Pulex (homeopathic) helps to soothe irritation.

Food hypersensitivity

Allergic reactions to some foods is not uncommon in cats. Some breeds such as the Oriental and Siamese often cannot tolerate dairy foods. Milk particularly can be a problem due to a lactose intolerance or the inability to absorb the sugar in milk. Proteins such as fish, beef, pork, lamb, chicken and eggs can also cause an immune reaction.
Symptoms: Skin irritation (nettle rash) will appear, especially around the head, neck and ears.
Treatment: If the sensitivity is not known, extensive testing will be necessary to determine the cause. Consult your vet for a suitable dietary regime. Calendula (herbal) tincture or cream, meanwhile, will soothe and cool irritation.

Pawnote:

An increasing amount of CFCs and other chemical pollutants invade our world today despite efforts to control these substances. A drug intolerance to various medicines, e.g. penicillin, can be the cause of an immune reaction, as can the fiber content of some carpeting materials. Certain primers, wood stain compositions and rubberised floor coverings are also toxic to cats.

Skin Problems

Signs and symptoms

Constant licking, scratching and subsequent hair loss will indicate a skin complaint.

Sunburn or solar dermatitis

Occurs when the white or light-colored cat with delicate pink skin has been exposed to ultra-violet light (UVB) from the sun for prolonged periods. Ear tips and margins of the eyelids, nose and lips can be affected. Solar dermatitis is a chronic, long-term condition which if left and irritating parts scratched by the cat can become cancerous.

Prevention: Avoid exposure to strong sunlight or apply water-proof SPF 20 plus sunblock.

Remedial action: Apply witch hazel cream to soothe and cool (herbal). Give Rescue Remedy in single drops if heatstroke is present (Bach Flower Remedy). Consult your vet to avoid deterioration of the condition.

Ringworm

A fungal skin infection, which is also transmissible to humans, caused by infection of hair, dead outer layers of skin and claws, and is passed on by contamination with an infected animal, infected bedding or grooming equipment. Long-haired cats are most at risk and infected patches can be seen – not always since some cats may carry ringworm but not show it – as circular or irregularly shaped patches containing scaling or dandruff.

Prevention: Keep your cat away from known sufferers – outbreaks in pedigrees are curbed by closing breeding catteries until all cats are clear.

Remedial action: Calendula ointment or Goldenseal or Echinacea tincture applied to affected parts once each day (herbal). Bacillinum, Tellurium, Sepia and Kali arsen (homeopathic). Consult your vet regarding treatment and disinfecting premises.

Alopecia

Alopecia is the loss or partial loss of hair, a symptom of what could be several underlying causes – the first being infestation by parasites where the skin has been bitten and scratched until bare patches appear. There could be an allergy to flea powder, food, plastic (feeding bowls) or other substances. Collars which may rub and irritate or contain flea repellent can cause hair loss. During pregnancy or lactation, queens may experience hair loss. Some aspects of FIV infection (see page 71) and ringworm (see above) can also cause alopecia.

Prevention: Not always possible since allergies are not evident until the symptoms occur. Early recognition of causes is essential to avoid distress. Flea and mite control is recommended.

Remedial action: Calendula (herbal) tincture or cream soothes and cools. Thallium (homeopathic) is a general hair restorer and Arsen. alb (Bio tissue salts) is for hair loss accompanied by itching. Consult your vet for advice and treatment.

Eczema
(feline miliary dermatitis)

Varying between mild or chronic, common causes are hypersensitivity to flea bites, parasitic infection, bacterial or yeast infection, allergies, immune suppressive-type diseases or skin contact with chemical substances. There is both "wet" (suppurating) eczema and "dry" (scaly) eczema.

Prevention: Prevention will follow symptomatic evidence, and forthwith all causal substances should be withheld.

Remedial action: Hypericum with Calendula tincture diluted as directed and applied directly onto affected parts. Apis mel. is ideal for allergic reactions; Cantharis for burning painful skin eruptions and Sulphur for hot itchy skin and to soothe flea bites (all homeopathic). Seek veterinary advice and treatment.

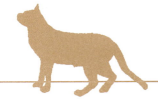

Reproductive Problems

Persistent calling can mean a medical problem.

Signs and symptoms

While cats do have a very efficient reproductive system, problems can be encountered in the un-neutered cat, male or female – more often the latter. Signs include:
- Failure to conceive after repeated matings
- Excessive periods of calling or "heat"
- Discharge from the vulva
- Obvious pregnancy which comes to nothing

Reasons for infertility

When mating has taken place and the queen fails or appears to fail to conceive, several reasons may be the cause. Has the queen had an accident and suffered an undetected miscarriage? Has she a uterine or vaginal infection? Pyometra? Ovarian cysts? Blocked fallopian tubes? Or perhaps she has a congenital absence or abnormality of her reproductive organs. Is there a nutritional deficiency, such as a lack of vitamin A, or perhaps she was not mated at the optimum period of her "heat" or oestrus.

Female infertility

The most likely and commonest cause is an infection in the reproductive system.
Symptom: A discharge from the vulva.
Treatment: Veterinary examination, diagnosis and treatment.

Male infertility

Cryptorchidism, where both testicles have not descended into the scrotum, is the most likely cause. In monorchidism, where only one of the testes has descended, a male cat can still be fertile. An infection of the reproductive system is common and could also be a cause of infertility, as can tumors of the testes. Obesity could inhibit a successful mating.
Symptoms: A discharge from the penis.
Treatment: Veterinary examination, diagnosis and treatment.

Ovarian cysts

Sometimes seen in a fertile queen that has not mated, these occur when ovarian follicles do not ripen but enlarge into cysts which produce large quantities of the female sex hormone.
Symptoms: Persistent calling, frequent or permanent heat periods, loss of condition and weight, discontented condition.

Treatment: Consult your vet for advice and possible hormone treatment.

Genital infection

Inflammation of the vagina can occur for a number of reasons – infection of the ovaries or fallopian tubes, a local infection in the vagina and an inflamed and infected vulva. An infection from a male cat while mating is also possible. The male can experience an infection of the spermatic cords, urethra and/or bladder or a local infection picked up in the litter tray or garden soil.
Symptoms: Small amounts of clear, serous discharge from the vagina (female) or penis (male), sometimes tinged with blood. More seriously, a discharge of blood and pus.
Treatment: Veterinary examination, diagnosis and treatment.

Metritis

A condition where acute or chronic infection of the uterus or womb follows a difficult birth – most likely to happen in the older or out of condition queen, where placental debris has been retained and/or there has been a Caesarean section or forceps birth. Infertility may arise following the chronic condition.
Symptoms: Loss of appetite, fever, abdominal pain and unpleasant discharge from the vulva.
Treatment: Consult your vet immediately if these signs are evident after kittening.

Respiratory Problems

Signs and symptoms

The cat's lungs, heart and circulatory system are designed to support the hunting animal in short, sharp bursts of physical activity, rapid reflex actions and instant hormonal response. Air is drawn in, making its way down the trachea (windpipe) into the lungs and through the two bronchi. Each of these splits off into the lesser bronchioles ending in small pockets called alveoli. When infection affects this area, you can expect these symptoms:

• Breathing difficulties, shallow or rapid
• Coughing and wheezing
• Coughs may be chesty and fluid/dry or harsh
• Discharge from eyes and nose

Call your vet immediately if your cat's respiration or breathing pattern is abnormal.

Persistent coughing or wheezing is an indication of respiratory problems.

Cat flu (feline upper respiratory disease)

Because of its extremely contagious nature, cat flu is one of the most common – and deadly – of all the feline infectious conditions (see page 70). Feline Calicivirus (FCV) and the more severe Feline Viral Rhinotracheitis (FVR), also known as feline herpesvirus (FHV-1), are the two main infectious causes. Cat flu is seen to worst and often fatal effect in the young kitten. Other less-known viruses exist which also cause feline respiratory disease.

Symptoms: Both FCV and FVR bring fever, sneezing, coughing, nasal discharge and weeping eyes. With Feline Calicivirus, tongue ulceration and paw lesions may also be present.

Treatment: Antibiotics will reduce severity of symptoms and the cat's own immune system will be a significant factor in its recovery.

Prevention: Vaccination against FCV and FVR is essential in the first instance.

Bronchitis

An inflammation of the lining mucous membrane of the air tubes or bronchioles, bronchitis may occur as an extension of inflammation of the trachea (tracheitis). This may be followed by pneumonia or pleurisy, or both. Both an acute and a chronic type of bronchitis are recognized.

Symptom: Mainly persistent coughing.

Treatment: Urgent veterinary supervision, careful nursing and controlled rest.

Prevention:
Vaccinations/boosters should be kept up to date to prevent respiratory disease and immune system well maintained.

Pleurisy

Pleurisy or pleuritis is a bacterial infection or inflammation of the pleura, the membrane covering the external surfaces of the lungs and cover of the inside of the chest walls. This may occur as a complication to pneumonia and/or other infections and occasionally from a chest wound. Friction between the inflamed surfaces causes pain as the cat breathes.

Symptoms: A change in the breathing pattern, fever, dullness and a rasping cough.

Treatment: As for bronchitis (see left and above).

Prevention: As for bronchitis.

Pneumonia

A condition in which there is an infection and/or inflammation of the lungs. This may follow severe respiratory disease, i.e. a viral/bacterial cause, or this may be due to parasites or inhaled foreign substances. Severity will be affected by the cat's immune system and its subsequent ability to fight off infection.

Symptoms: Lethargy, rapid, painful and shallow breathing, coughing, nasal discharge and fever.

Treatment: Urgent veterinary supervision, careful nursing and controlled rest.

Prevention: FCV and FVR vaccinations/boosters should be kept up to date and immune system well maintained to combat general infection.

Pleuro-pneumonia

This is a combination of pleurisy and pneumonia. Acute pneumonia, often accompanied by pleurisy, will account for the extreme chest pain that the cat experiences when breathing.

Symptoms: As for pleurisy and pneumonia.

Treatment: As for pneumonia.

Prevention: As for pneumonia.

Lungworm

The lungworm is a small roundworm 7-9 mm (about 3/8 in) long and is found in the terminal bronchioles and the pulmonary artery of the lung (see page 79). It is greyish-white in colour and slender with tapered end parts. The hunting cat becomes infected by eating birds, molluscs (slugs and snails) or rodents carrying lungworm larvae.

Symptoms: Often none, but there may be a persistent, dry cough, lethargy, lack of appetite and weight loss.

Treatment: Consult your vet for appropriate treatment.

Prevention: None unless the hunting cat is restricted to an indoor lifestyle.

Asthma

A condition which may be applied to an allergic reaction in response to a particular substance, causing spasmodic expulsion of breath without the effort of a cough. The true spasmodic asthma is of nervous origin and due to a sudden distressful contraction of the muscle fibers which lie around the smaller bronchioles. In some cases, asthma may be an allergic phenomenon. In other instances, a chronic inflammation of the mucous membrane lining of the small tubes is the case. In the allergenic asthma attack, the cause is often botanical and gives rise to seasonal (summer and autumn) attacks.

Bronchial asthma

Sometimes known as allergic bronchitis, this condition can be caused by pollens, house dust, mites or a variety of other substances your cat may encounter inside or outside the home.

Symptoms: Sudden wheezing attacks of perhaps a dry, progressing to a loose, wet coughing. Cats who have had respiratory disease in the past are more likely to suffer more severely due to mucous membrane lining damage in the bronchioles.

Treatment: Urgent veterinary diagnosis (isolation of the cause) is required. Treatment could include antibiotics, cortisone and antihistamines. Eucalyptus, given by massage or by diffuser, will ease breathing. NEVER massage pure oils into the skin. Dilute as instructed.

Atopic disease

A hypersensitivity to substances in the cat's environment, i.e. house dust, house-dust mites, human skin/dandruff and pollen.

Symptoms: As in bronchial asthma, but can also include sneezing, conjunctivitis and rhinitis.

Treatment: Take your cat to the vet as soon as symptoms are noticed. On isolation of the cause, eradication and future avoidance of the substance concerned will be necessary. Treatment could include steroids and antihistamines with additional natural-oil preparations.

Urinary Problems

Signs and symptoms

The urinary system maintains a correct balance of chemicals in the blood; it retains useful ones and eliminates toxic ones. Toxic waste passes through the kidneys which then release this as urine. The urine passés down the ureters to the bladder, through the urethra and then exits the body via the penis (male) or the vulva (female). From urinary infection to kidney disease, symptoms of problems can appear to be similar. It is important to investigate underlying causes. Signs to watch out for are:

- Difficulty and discomfort in passing small amounts of urine
- Blood-tinged urine
- Cloudy or discolored urine
- Excessive thirst/more frequent urination than usual
- Inappropriate urination/"accidents" indoors when generally of clean habits

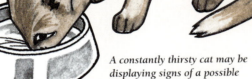

A constantly thirsty cat may be displaying signs of a possible urinary problem

Warning:
Seek immediate veterinary advice if any of these symptoms occur. Delay could be life-threatening or fatal.

Cystitis

Cystitis is inflammation of the inner lining of the bladder. In male cats, this can be associated with Feline Urological Syndrome (FUS) and is also the case in females where there is contamination of the vulva by defecation, when bacteria travels up the urethra to the bladder.

Symptoms: Frequent urination and straining while doing so, varying degrees of blood-tinged urine, pungent odor to the urine, persistent licking of the genital area.

Treatment: Your vet may take a sample of the cat's urine to determine the particular bacteria and so prescribe correct antibiotics. The condition should respond favorably to the antibiotics. If allowed to deteriorate, however, the bladder may become blocked. Increase and encourage fluid (water) intake and eliminate all dry foods from the cat's diet.

Prevention: Hygienic precau-tions with litter trays, offer plenty of clean water at all times and give only dry food or biscuits occasionally.

Kidney disease

Diet and physical inactivity can be triggering factors in kidney disease, although failing kidneys are generally age-related and often afflict the elderly cat. However, kidneys which deteriorate in their ability to function correctly can occur as a result of injury, diabetes or follow Feline

Infectious Peritonitis (FIP), a disease affecting the liver, kidneys and nervous system. Kidney disease can be seen in the chronic or in the less severe acute form. The former usually affects the elderly cat while the latter, less common type affects the younger cat, and in both the young and old, causes can include swallowing a toxic substance.

Symptoms: Chronic – more frequent urination than usual, excessive thirst, weight loss, lethargy and depression, poor coat condition, anemia, foul breath and some vomiting. Acute – loss of appetite, vomiting, depression and dehydration.

Treatment: Chronic – immediate veterinary advice required. Following clinical examination, urine and blood tests are undergone to determine the extent of kidney damage. Good dietary management under veterinary supervision (he or she may recommend a specially formulated food). If the condition is not attended to, toxic waste will build up with fatal results. Acute – immediate veterinary advice required. If a toxic substance is involved, remedial action should be taken and plenty of fluids given.

Prevention: Plenty of exercise, maintain a "plenty of clean, fresh water at all times" policy and do not offer a dry food-only diet. Avoid contact with cats suffering from Feline Infectious Peritonitis (FIP). Secure away all toxic substances.

Incontinence

Loss of control of the bladder can be a symptom of infection of the bladder, injury or old age. Spraying or territory marking urination should not be confused with incontinence. Consult your vet immediately, especially if there are other symptoms such as straining or if the urine is blood-stained. Water intake should not be limited.

Feline Urological Syndrome (FUS)

Also referred to as feline urolithiasis, this condition is common and can be fatal in both the male and female cat. Inflammation of the bladder and urethra, plus the formation of sand-like crystals (struvite) or a sandy sludge, can cause blockage of the bladder and effectively "plug" the urethra. This can particularly affect the male neutered cat since the urethra in this case is long, narrow and curved.

Symptoms: Straining to pass urine which can be blood-stained, distended bladder with tense and painful abdomen, crying in pain if touched in that area, lack of appetite and excessive licking of genital area.

Treatment: Consult your vet immediately to clear the obstruction, by passing a catheter up the urethra and into the bladder of the anesthetized cat. A blocked urethra can be fatal due to toxic build-up or rupture. Dietary control is essential – no dry foods. Increase water intake.

Prevention: Always leave a bowl of clean, fresh water for your cat to drink at any time. Ensure there is not an excess of dry food or magnesium in the diet (proprietary canned foods state percentage contained). Allow plenty of exercise.

Feline lower urinary tract disease (FLUTD)

This is a syndrome rather than a condition and affects the lower urinary tract, i.e. the bladder and urethra. It is generally seen to involve cystitis or inflammation of the inner lining of the bladder and degrees of blockage of the urethra.

Symptoms, treatment and prevention: As for cystitis and FUS. Veterinary treatment is essential.

Neurological Problems

Signs and symptoms

The cat's intricate nervous system co-ordinates and controls all aspects of its life. Working in two directions, a network of information via the sensory nerves informs the cat's brain how it feels, and the motor nerves carry this information from the brain to tell the cat's body how to respond. While the central nervous system is well protected from possible trauma, the outer nerves are vulnerable to damage. Should the cat's nervous system be affected, these are signs that you will notice:

• Lack of coordination
• Dilated pupils
• Vomiting and regurgitation of food
• Seizures
• Fits or epilepsy
• Paralysis

cat's eyes showing dilated pupils

Loss of balance

General unsteadiness and lack of co-ordination when walking can be caused by several factors – a fault in the development of the cat, injury, a vitamin deficiency or an inner ear infection. Viral infections such as feline infectious peritonitis (FIP) and panleucopenia virus and some poisons or parasites can damage nerves.

Symptoms: Unsteadiness and a weaving gait; head held to one side.

Treatment: Seek veterinary advice immediately to determine the cause of the problem and relevant treatment.

Brain damage

The most common cause of brain damage – severe trauma to the head – is by road traffic accident or a fall. Strokes or cerebral hemorrhages can occur as a result of a blood clot and these can cause paralysis or decreased function in parts of the body. Other reasons for brain damage can be bacterial infection, tumours or a traumatic birth. The result is often fatal.

Symptoms: Decreased activity, drowsiness or paralysis of limbs or tail. Loss of sight.

Treatment: Urgent veterinary treatment is essential. While cats can recover from minor strokes, other side-effects such as fits or epilepsy may need to be dealt with.

Paralysis

This may be due to serious brain damage and/or cerebral hemorrhage, or there may be a localized paralysis, usually as a result of an accident and happening most frequently to a limb or tail. The damaged appendage may drag on the floor as the cat moves around.

Symptoms: As for brain damage.

Treatment: If treatment of the affected part does not yield successful results within a month, amputation is often considered necessary to prevent ulceration and infection.

Fits or epilepsy

Often connected with brain damage, fits (convulsions) and epilepsy do not often occur in cats. Other than brain damage, causes can be an inherited defect, poisoning or a vitamin deficiency. These can begin in kittenhood or may suddenly occur following an accident or injury to the head.

Symptoms: The cat will lie on its side unconscious, twitching, gnashing its teeth and frothing at the mouth. Its legs will be threshing and paddling around.

Treatment: Do not touch the cat. Resist the urge to try to stop it swallowing its tongue with your fingers – you could receive a severe bite. Darken the room and keep all as quiet as possible. If the convulsion has not stopped after five minutes, carefully lift the cat by the scruff of the neck, place it in its carrier and take it to the vet immediately. If this cannot be done, telephone your vet for assistance. If the fit is brief (under five minutes), stay with your cat and then take it to your vet.

Meningitis

Inflammation affecting the membranes covering the brain (cerebral meningitis), the spinal cord (spinal meningitis) or both (cerebrospinal meningitis). This condition is generally associated with viral or bacterial diseases.

Symptoms: Fever, restlessness, dilated pupils, loss of appetite and convulsions.

Treatment: Urgent veterinary treatment is essential. Spinal fluid may be taken for examination. If the meningitis follows a head injury, the skull should be examined for fractures. Keep the cat in a quiet, darkened room.

Encephalitis

Inflammation of the brain which can be caused by some viruses such as rabies, fungi or bacterial infection.

Symptoms: The symptoms are similar to meningitis, plus delirium, convulsions and loss of consciousness.

Treatment: Urgent veterinary treatment is essential. The cause of the infection needs to be established. Avoid handling the cat and keep it in a quiet darkened room.

Feline Dysautonomia (Key-Gaskell Syndrome)

A rare disease and only recognised during 1981-82, causes of the Key-Gaskell Syndrome are at present unknown.

Symptoms: Depression, dilated pupils which are unresponsive to light, loss of appetite, prominent nictitating membranes ("third" eyelid, see page 76), weight loss, vomiting, regurgitation of food and constipation and diarrhea in some cases. Also, there may be some difficulty in swallowing food due to an enlargement of the esophagus.

Treatment: Urgent veterinary treatment is essential. Dehy-

dration to be countered by means of a glucose-saline solution fed by drip and liquid foods by syringe, if necessary.

Poisoning

Many household chemicals, medicines, other indoor and outdoor hazards and plant substances are poisonous to cats. (see pages 40-41).

Symptoms: General symptoms are convulsions, muscle tremors and vomiting.

Treatment: Once you have confirmed that your cat has eaten or come into contact with a poisonous substance, contact the vet immediately. Meanwhile, save the container containing the poison so that the vet can treat accordingly. If the hair or skin is contaminated by a toxic substance, do not remove with spirits, gas or solvents. Dissolve contamination and/or wash the coat using a baby shampoo or one especially prepared for cats. Pay particular attention to bare skin areas such as nose, ear flaps, under the tail and paw pads. Poison can be absorbed into the system via the skin. If the cat is having convulsions, contact your vet immediately and see left for care regarding fits and convulsions.

Blood Disorders

spread via the saliva of an infected cat (see also page 71).

Signs and symptoms

Signs of disorders with the blood and circulatory system are:

- Anemia
- Weight loss
- Pallor and/or bluish tinge to the gums
- Lethargy and weakness
- Paralysis

Feline Leukaemia Virus (FeLV)

Cancer of the white blood cells and lymphosarcoma or cancer of the lymph glands. It can involve the intestine or other organs. Extremely contagious and most common in multi-cat house-holds, all cats are susceptible (see also pages 70-71).

Symptoms: Not specific, but a variety of infections and diseases may become evident due to lowered immune system. Weight loss, anemia, vomiting and diarrhea.

Treatment: Blood tests to iden-tify the virus. There is no specif-ic cure, although a vaccine is available. Appropriate treatment will relieve the various sec-ondary problems.

Feline Immunodeficiency Virus (FIV)

Causing a similar effect to the HIV virus in humans, FIV results in immunosuppression and the inability to combat infection and disease. It is

Symptoms: Onset of the disease is similar to FeLV; non-specific and with the cat being "off-color." Secondary infections develop owing to immunosup-pression – anemia, weight loss, loss of appetite, fluctuation in temperature and swollen glands (lymph nodes).

Treatment: Blood tests to iden-tify the virus. There is no specif-ic cure. Secondary infection and problems can be treated and nursed but FIV positive cats are a health risk to other cats.

Anemia

Anemia is caused by a shortage of the hemoglobin or red blood cells, thereby reducing the amount of oxygen carried in the blood. Anemia is not a disease and it is therefore necessary to discover the causal factors. Causes could include contact with poison, such as lead, para-sites, immunity reaction, i.e. via blood transfusion, accident and loss of blood, dietary deficiency, and so on.

Symptoms: Lethargy, weakness, loss of appetite and pallor of the gums.

Treatment: Consult your vet immediately for diagnosis.

Feline Infectious Anaemia (FIA)

Caused by a small blood parasite transmitted by the flea or tick and which attaches itself to the wall of red blood cells, causing their destruction and subsequent anaemic condition of the cat.

Symptoms: High temperature, loss of appetite and weight loss, lethargy and mucous mem-branes are pale and, in advanced conditions, jaundiced.

Treatment: Consult your vet as soon as possible. Blood tests will determine the condition. Specific antibiotics, multi-vita-mins (iron supplements) and a blood transfusion may be given.

Blood tests

In order to identify some feline diseases and conditions, such as Feline Leukaemia Virus (FeLV), Feline Immuno Deficiency Virus (FIV), Infectious Feline Anaemia (FIV) and in the general anaemic condition, blood tests will need to be taken by your vet. In the case of a road traffic accident where there is severe blood loss, your cat's blood type will need to be identified before a blood transfusion takes place. There are three main blood groups in the feline and these are A, B and AB. Most cats are type A.

Heart problems

There are several types of heart conditions and problems which affect the cat, including congenital defects such as holes in the heart walls or a deterioration of the heart muscle. Most kittens born with these defects die during their first year. Infection, too, such as feline upper respiratory disease (cat flu, see page 70) can cause damage to the heart and also illnesses such as pneumonia and pleurisy (see pages 88-89). Problems are much more common with the advancing years – heart valves may become diseased, get blocked or grow weaker.

Symptoms: Difficulty in breathing, irregular heartbeats, breathlessness during exertion, a bluish tinge to the gums and there could be some swelling around the chest area. A dryish cough could indicate valvular disease.

Treatment: Consult your vet immediately if you notice the above conditions. The vet will listen to your cat's heart with a stethoscope and perhaps carry out x-rays or blood tests to make a diagnosis. Depending upon the particular heart problem involved, drugs can be prescribed for some conditions. Regular check-ups are advised.

Cardiomyopathy

This condition is a significant cause of heart failure in cats. Hypertrophic cardiomyopathy is associated with the thickening of the heart muscle mass which encloses the left ventricle of the heart. The left ventricle, one of the two larger chambers of the heart, pumps blood through the aorta or main artery and hypertrophy of the left ventricle leads to heart failure. Dilated cardiomyopathy can occur in cats deficient in taurine, an essential amino-acid. A taurine deficiency can also lead to degeneration of the cat's retina and possible blindness.

Symptoms: Lethargy and weakness, loss of appetite, weight loss, abdominal swelling and breathing difficulties. There can be clotting of blood in the hind legs and some pain.

Treatment: Consult your vet immediately if you notice the above symptoms. To lessen the strain on the heart, treatment will include removing fluid build-up in lungs, chest or others sites where it has accumulated. Surgery may be used to unblock arteries of the hind legs. Taurine supplementation will be given if a deficiency is suspected (see page 28).

Thrombosis

This condition is brought on when a blood vessel is blocked by a blood clot and cuts off the blood supply. It may follow atheroma or injury to a blood vessel. In cats, thrombosis of the femoral arteries is not uncommon and causes paralysis of the hind legs with some pain. An iliac thrombosis occurs in the aorta or main artery. Reasons for this can be a portion of diseased heart valve tissue travelling through the bloodstream to become blocked in the aorta.

Symptoms: These develop suddenly and decisively giving shock, pain, collapse and partial or total paralysis to the hind legs which will feel very cold to the touch. The pulse in the femoral arteries area (see above) will be absent.

Treatment: Urgent veterinary treatment is essential. Surgery can sometimes unblock the blood vessel(s) concerned but recovery rate is not high.

Heartworm

See page 79.

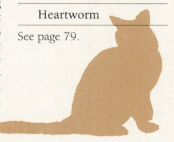

Nursing a Sick Cat

Peace and quiet

Recovery following sickness, injury or an operation will be speeded along if you give your cat lots of loving care in surroundings that are both familiar and reassuring to it. Place your sick cat in a safe, quiet place, preferably in a darkened room and away from the rest of the family – including other pets!

Keeping warm

It is essential to keep your sick cat warm, especially during the night when temperatures drop considerably and the resistance of a poorly cat is often at a low ebb. In cases of vomiting, diarrhoea or incontinence, make a draught-free bed from a deep-sided cardboard box with a cut-out piece in one side to allow access to a litter tray, if the cat is able to do this. In the hygiene-conscious cat, maintaining normal litter-tray habits is important.

Line the bottom of the box with layers of newspaper and place on top of this a piece of warm, absorbent vet-bed, or thick folded towels. Place a half-filled rubber hot water bottle, wrapped in a small sheet or towelling between newspaper and vet-bed to keep your cat warm and cosy. Ensure that the bottle is not too hot and does not come into direct contact with your cat's body.

An ambient warmth can be obtained with a low-wattage infra-red lamp. Use microwaveable pads and low-wattage heated pads to introduce heat quickly. Both should be placed well under the existing bedding.

Feeding

Loss of appetite is a natural symptom in most sick cats. This is often counterbalanced by a need for fluids, especially where there are diarrhea or kidney problems. Certain illnesses, such as feline lower urinary tract disease (FLUTD), require specially formulated food prescribed by your vet.

For the cat that refuses food or is too weak to eat, force-feeding of liquidized food by syringe is the only answer. For one who has lost his appetite, spoon-feeding small amounts of strong-smelling foods such as finely mashed sardines or pilchards may encourage it to eat. Yeast extract or liquidized beef or chicken broth may tempt the sick cat. Feed little and often.

Food should always be warmed to blood temperature.

Feed protein-rich foods to aid recovery, such as fish, light meat, scrambled egg yolk or egg yolk beaten into skimmed milk and fed by spoon. If your cat does accept eggs, never feed egg white. Albumin itself is a protein but is associated with causing inflammation of the kidneys.

Importance of fluids

While a cat can survive for some time without solid food, fluids need to be given to avoid dehydration, especially when vomiting or diarrhea are present. Try a little honey dissolved in warm water and allowed to cool to a lukewarm temperature. If your cat is too ill to respond to the spoon, try dripping the liquid into the corner of the mouth with a dropper.

Diets for convalescing cats

There are specially formulated proprietary brands of food for convalescing cats. Ask your vet about these – they are generally available from the surgery.

Home-made recipes

Lightly textured food, such as minced chicken or lean beef, brown rice and chopped or grated vegetables, can be mixed and lightly cooked. Blend these ingredients in a blender. For the convalescing adult or elderly cat, think "kitten" and feed the type of food you would offer a small needful kitten. Feed as necessary in order to maintain or regain weight lost.

Nursing Kit

- A sheet of bubble wrap and heat-generating pads
- Cotton wool
- Disposable gloves
- Disinfectant, i.e. hydrogen peroxide or tea tree oil – dilute as per instructions
- Salt for bathing wounds
- Thermometer
- Syringe
- Eye dropper
- Dosing gun
- Arnica (for bruising)
- Rescue remedy (for trauma and shock)
- Moist face-wipes

Supplements

Add cod fish-liver oil to food as a source of vitamins A and D (do not give higher than directed amounts for long periods) and small amounts of bone-meal for calcium (as sold for human use, not the type sold for garden use). Kelp powder or multi-mineral kelp tablets can be grated onto food. Wheat germ oil works best when the capsules are broken open over food. In the same way, Vitamin E capsules can be used with the wheat germ oil and served on food.

Grooming a sick cat

A little gentle grooming will help boost your poorly friend's morale, as well as keeping it clean and comfortable. If you feel your cat is really too ill to be lifted onto your knee or a table for grooming, simply hand-groom or brush the coat gently as the cat lies in its bed.

Hind quarters: In the case of incontinence and diarrhoea, gently wipe around the anal area with damp cotton wool swabs and dry carefully with dry ones. Clean tail fur, if necessary, with warm water containing a light solution of tea tree oil and dry carefully and thoroughly.

Coat: When your cat vomits, immediately wipe the mouth and contaminated fur with dampened cotton wool swabs (a clean one for each wipe), so that the vomit does not dry on the fur.

Eyes: With special antiseptic "eye wipes" or dampened cotton wool swabs, clean the eye from the outside to the inside nearest to the nose. Never use the same swab twice.

Nose: By the same method, gently clean the nostrils and dry with a clean swab.

Mouth: Keep the mouth clean of dribbles or vomit in the same way. For the convalescing or injured cat which is bed-bound but moderately perky, try cleaning his or her teeth with a toothbrush and toothpaste in the normal way (see pages 44-45).

Giving Medicine

When the time comes to take its medicine, no creature is more crafty than the cat. Persistence and a firm, friendly manner is the order of the day. Because the cat naturally pushes its tongue outwards when lapping liquid or eating food, unwanted medicine, if placed on the tongue, will tend to be expelled with some force from the mouth – unless you are prepared.

Tablets

1. Place the cat on a firm, raised, non-slip surface and gently enclose the head between the fingers of your left hand. Tilt the head backwards slightly.

2. Take the tablet in your right hand and open the cat's mouth with the fingers of the same hand.

3. Place the tablet firmly but gently as far back as possible onto the cat's tongue (see right).

4. Close the jaws and hold them together for a few moments. Gently stroke under the chin to encourage the cat to swallow the tablet.

Liquids

1. Position the cat on a firm, raised, non-slip surface and tilt back the head as for taking tablets.

2. Take the spoonful of medicine in your right hand and gently prise open the cat's jaws with the last two fingers of the same hand.

3. Swiftly place the spoon into the cat's mouth as far back as

---

Pawnote:

Some gun or pill-popper manufacturers recommend adding water to help the pill along its way. This is not advisable since there could be a danger of choking if the water accidentally squirted into the cat's windpipe.

---

possible, turning it over in the mouth as you do so. This is necessary because the cat's tongue will be pushing out the medicine at the same time. Wearing an overall or plastic apron is a good idea!

4. With all possible speed, close the cat's jaws and hold them together for a couple of seconds. When the cat has finished gulping and swallowing, gently stroke under the chin, thus ensuring that all the medicine has gone down the throat.

The struggling cat

If your cat struggles or is aggressive, wrap him firmly in a thick towel so that all flailing legs are restrained.

1. Position yourself behind the cat, place the towel over the cat's back and quickly pick him up. Meanwhile, swiftly wrap the towel around the body.

2. With your cat safely lodged

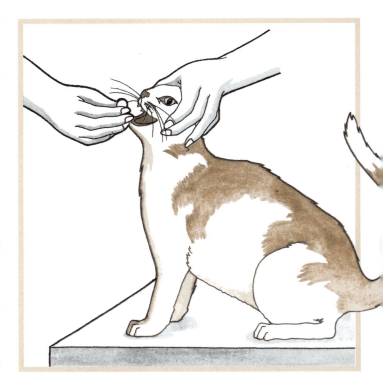

under your left arm and with your left hand tilting back the cat's head, hold him by the scruff of the neck and proceed to administer tablet or liquid medication with your right hand.

3. Gently close the mouth and stroke under the chin several times ensuring that the medication has gone down the throat.

Tips for disguising medicine

• Tablets which are dry and powdery will probably slip down the throat more easily if coated with a little butter or margarine.

• Large tablets may be more acceptable if they are broken into halves or quarters. Take care that no crumbs are left, otherwise your cat will not be getting the required dose.

• If you sprinkle on or mix the medicine with food, make sure the meal is only a very small portion, otherwise if the food is left, the full strength of medication will not be taken.

Using a dosing gun

For the experienced cat owner, another way to give a tablet to your cat is by way of a dosing gun. These can be obtained from your vet. Open the cat's mouth and tilt the head back slightly, as previously shown, and then fire the tablet into the back of the cat's mouth. Close the mouth and gently stroke the throat, ensuring that the tablet goes down.

Using a syringe

You may need some assistance with this method of administering liquid medicine to your cat. An extra pair of hands from behind will be very useful to steady the forelegs. Hold the cat's head with your hand and tilt back slightly, as previously shown, placing the syringe into the side of the cat's mouth. Your cat will probably start to chew on the syringe so that the liquid will then be swallowed. When all the medication has been taken, remove the syringe, gently close the cat's mouth and smooth the throat to ensure that all has gone down. Clean the mouth area with a damp swab.

Giving an injection

Though normally administered by the vet, should daily injections need to be given, as would be the case with diabetes, then your vet will show you how to carry out this routine for yourself. Your vet will also provide the necessary sterile syringes for the job. Again, place the patient on a firm, raised, non-slip surface and hold it by the scruff or loose skin at the back of its neck. Lift up the skin away from the body, insert the needle into it (see left) and slowly inject the medication.

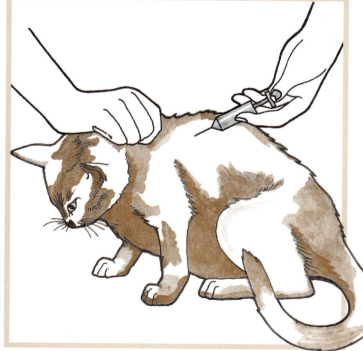

Giving Eye and Ear Drops

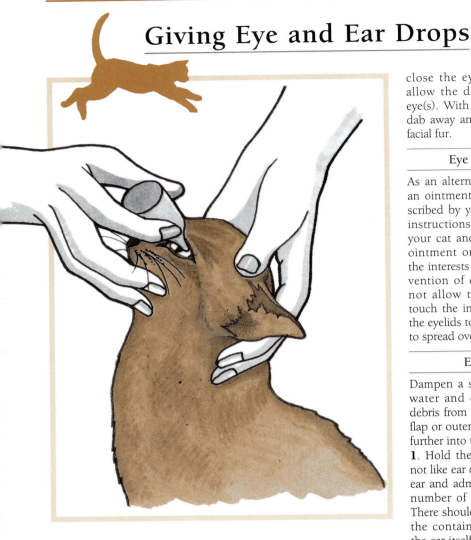

close the eyelids carefully to allow the drops to bathe the eye(s). With a dry swab, lightly dab away any residue from the facial fur.

Eye ointments

As an alternative to eye drops, an ointment is sometimes prescribed by your vet. Follow the instructions above for holding your cat and squeeze a line of ointment onto the eyeball. In the interests of hygiene and prevention of cross-infection, do not allow the tube nozzle to touch the infected eye(s). Close the eyelids to allow the ointment to spread over the eye(s).

Ear drops

Dampen a swab with sterilised water and clean away dirt or debris from the inside of the ear flap or outer ear. Do not intrude further into the ear.
1. Hold the cat firmly (cats do not like ear drops), fold back the ear and administer the required number of drops into the ear. There should be no necessity for the container nozzle to touch the ear itself. For more than one cat requiring ear drops at the same time, sterilize the nozzle after dosing each cat.
2. Close and gently massage the ear flap to ensure the drops remain inside the ear.

Eye drops

1. Place the cat on a raised, firm, non-slip surface. When either one or both eyes are affected, position yourself to face the cat.
2. Using a clean swab dampened in sterilized water, bathe the eye(s) from the outside to the inside edge nearest the nose to remove any discharge. To avoid cross-infection, use a clean swab for each eye.

3. For dealing with a single eye infection, gently but firmly clasp the cat's head with one hand, cupping the unaffected side with your thumb around the bottom jaw to keep it closed. For both eyes, hold the back of the cat's head firmly and with two fingers of the hand give the eye drops while gently steadying the jaw.
4. Apply the required number of drops to the eyeball itself. Tilt your cat's head back slightly and

General Nursing

Sometimes, surgery is required to be performed on the ailing or injured cat. This will be carried out at the veterinary surgery and following the operation, while the patient is recovering from the anesthetic, your vet will instruct you on the necessary post-operative care for your cat.

On your arrival home, set up the cat in a quiet, warm and secluded "sick area." Ensure that the cat-flap is locked and that the invalid is safely confined indoors. Following an operation, the patient must be kept warm, so place a warmed hot water bottle in the bed (see page 96). When the cat has recovered from the anesthetic completely, encourage him to eat a light meal and keep a bowl of fresh clean water nearby. If you notice any worrying change in your cat's condition, call the vet immediately.

Recovery

Unless they are elderly, suffer from heart problems or are in some way vulnerable to the anesthetic, cats generally pull through an operation and the recovery outlook is good. They generally adapt to broken or amputated legs, loss of tail and other physical impediments very quickly. Following an operation, stitches will be removed by the vet or, if dissolvable, totally dissolve within 7-10 days.

Caring for wounds

Before leaving for home, the vet will have shown you how to care for – and protect – your cat's wounds. For instance:

Bandages: If your cat has a dressed wound, he or she will do their utmost to remove the dressing to lick the wound – another throwback to the wild where animals lick their wounds clean with their own healing saliva. So that stitches remain intact, e.g. on a leg wound, wrap an elastic bandage not too tightly but tight enough to prevent removal by the cat around the leg.

Female spaying (altering)/ male castration (neutering): Both of these operations are carried out under general anesthetic. In the case of the female, no dressing is necessary for this operation. A spray-on dressing may be applied, however, to prevent nibbling at the stitches. The female will be a "walking-wounded" case and recovery should be complete within several days. Male neutering involves removal of the testes. No stitches are usually required and recovery should be complete within 48 hours.

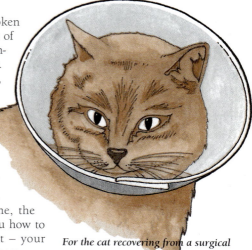

For the cat recovering from a surgical wound or irritating skin condition, it is important that these parts are protected from being licked, nibbled or scratched. An Elizabethan collar will help prevent this.

Herbal remedies

Herbal and homeopathic remedies can aid the recovery of your cat after an operation.

Rescue Remedy (Bach flower remedy) for trauma and shock.

Aconite (homeopathic) for trauma and shock.

Garlic (herbal) – an antiseptic used internally and externally.

Tea Tree Oil lotion (herbal and used externally), diluted, also an antiseptic.

Marigold lotion (herbal and for external use) for abscesses and/or infection.

Garlic, Nettle, Echinacea (herbal and for internal use) for abscesses and/or if infection develops in a wound.

Chlorella – a green algae, rich in vitamins and minerals (internal), for healing damaged tissue.

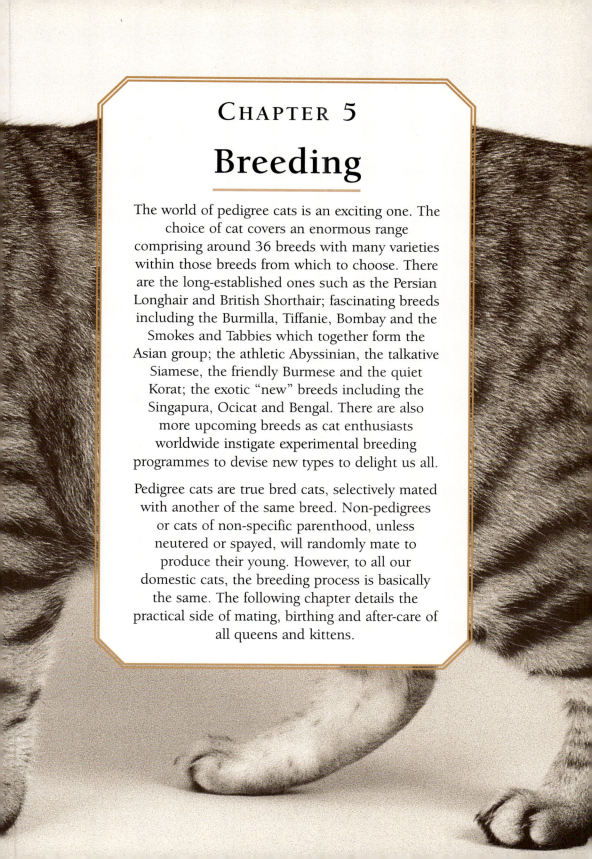

CHAPTER 5

Breeding

The world of pedigree cats is an exciting one. The choice of cat covers an enormous range comprising around 36 breeds with many varieties within those breeds from which to choose. There are the long-established ones such as the Persian Longhair and British Shorthair; fascinating breeds including the Burmilla, Tiffanie, Bombay and the Smokes and Tabbies which together form the Asian group; the athletic Abyssinian, the talkative Siamese, the friendly Burmese and the quiet Korat; the exotic "new" breeds including the Singapura, Ocicat and Bengal. There are also more upcoming breeds as cat enthusiasts worldwide instigate experimental breeding programmes to devise new types to delight us all.

Pedigree cats are true bred cats, selectively mated with another of the same breed. Non-pedigrees or cats of non-specific parenthood, unless neutered or spayed, will randomly mate to produce their young. However, to all our domestic cats, the breeding process is basically the same. The following chapter details the practical side of mating, birthing and after-care of all queens and kittens.

Planning to Breed

The breeding cycle

Male cats enter the mating game at an earlier stage than do most females – at around four months of age.

Female cats, according to type and breed, differ slightly in age in their mating activity. Non-pedigrees are generally ready to reproduce at around four to six months of age. However, it is generally thought that early mating is not good for a female, since she is insufficiently mature to deal with kittens both physically and in a behavioral context.

Over-affectionate; begins to call; rubs against objects; rolls from side to side on the floor; vulva becomes pink and enlarged

Dec 27

Dec 31

Jan 2

Jan 4

Ideal time for mating is within 48 hours of peak period

Queen will now have resumed normal behavior pattern

Individual queens vary in their length of "call." The above is a general sample of a queen's behavior from beginning to end of the estrus cycle

Gestation

The gestation period can vary from 62-65 days.

Breeders may find it useful to observe their queen's behavior and frequency of heat periods and make an appropriate chart. After mating, a gestation table chart indicating the expected date of birth is also a vital source of information (see example below).

Signs of estrus

Some queens do not advertise their estrus with the same enthusiasm as others. For instance, many non-pedigree cats have a very quiet voice, relying more heavily on scent. In the pedigree world, Persian Longhairs, Korats and others have tiny voices, so it is up to the owner to ensure their cat does not escape at these times.

General signs of estrus are restlessness and displays of over-affection, with the female rubbing against your legs or any upright object, often rear end first. She will lie on the floor and roll from side to side. The vulva itself will become increasingly pink, damp and swollen, and you will notice her continually washing away a clear discharge.

Choosing a mate

For the pedigree breeding queen, this will have been organised well before estrus sets in. Even during kittenhood, plans can be made. Suitable males of her own breed will be sought by perusing bloodlines and type. Choosing a male from the queen's own bloodline is not a good idea. If each cat carries a defective gene, defects hitherto hidden may suddenly spring to life.

Visit cat shows, talk to owners of suitable studs, read breed and breeding books and peruse the cat press. Bear in mind that queens visit studs, and those that have to travel long distances by road or rail can often go off call. If all comes to nothing, a genuine breeder/stud owner will accept a fee for the first attempt with subsequent efforts free of charge.

Gestation Table

January

Mating	1	2	3	4	5	6	7	8	9	10	11	12	13	14	15	16
Kittens	7	8	9	10	11	12	13	14	15	16	17	18	19	20	21	22

March

January

Mating	17	18	19	20	21	22	23	24	25	26	27	28	29	30	31
Kittens	23	24	25	26	27	28	29	30	31	1	2	3	4	5	6

March   **April**

February

Mating	1	2	3	4	5	6	7	8	9	10	11	12	13	14
Kittens	7	8	9	10	11	12	13	14	15	16	17	18	19	20

April

For instance, a queen mated on January 1 should have her kittens on March 7.

Mating

The visiting queen

When the queen arrives at the home of the stud, she will need a litter box, refreshment and rest, probably in that order. In the stud house will be a comfortable queen's quarters, separated from the stud's quarters by a fine wire partition, through which he can observe his visitor, and pick up her scent.

When the stud's owner feels that the queen is ready, she will be released into the stud pen. If all is well, the queen will allow the male to sniff her hindquarters and then she will flatten her body to the ground, raise her haunches in a "lordosis" position and "tread" her hind legs vigorously while presenting herself to the male. He will circle around the queen waiting for the propitious moment to mount her.

The stud will then grasp the female firmly by the scruff of the neck, a position assumed by approaching the female from the side as well as from behind. The experienced queen will accommodate the male by holding her tail to one side to allow the male to achieve his object.

Copulation is of short duration and as soon as this is completed, the stud will leap to one side away from the queen which, with a piercing cry, may attack the male. She will roll about from side to side, thrashing her tail, perhaps

for several minutes longer. When the stud owner sees this, she will temporarily remove the stud from the enclosure since he may try to mate the queen again. Never attempt to touch the queen at this time, since this could be dangerous with hands and arms ending up being severely scratched.

A single mating does not always result in kittens and second and third matings should complete the length of the queen's visit and also see the end of her "peak period."

Aftercare

On her return home, the queen should be put in a quiet spot away from the family and any other household pets.

Up-to-date vaccination certificates are required to be seen by the stud owner and those of the stud should be seen by the owner of the queen, so that, generally, major disease and infections can be ruled out. But the queen's immune system may well be slightly weakened after mating and she could, therefore, "shed" any bacteria and minor infection already in her system to the possible danger of other cats in the household.

Other cats in the household may also be disturbed by the varying scents now surrounding the queen (including that of the stud). Neuters and entire cats alike may misread the messages and fights could ensue. Until the just-mated queen has completely gone past her estrus and, scent-wise, has returned to comparative normality, she should be kept apart from the others.

Meanwhile, the queen needs light, nourishing food and plenty of fresh clean water to be available at all times, plus the avoidance of stress which could induce an often unnoticed abortion or re-sorption (mummification of the fetus).

Pregnancy

Signs of pregnancy

During the first fortnight of her return from the stud, the queen's nipples will pink up if she is pregnant, she will demand more food, have a more affectionate nature and become increasingly docile and broody.

Allow the pregnant mum to explore the house for one or more nest sites. As the time wears on, there will be much tearing up and shredding of available paper.

Care of the pregnant cat

Nutrition: Ensuring a good, nutritional diet is essential for the pregnant queen, containing sufficient calcium, minerals and vitamins. If she obviously requires them, increase the number of meals given but make them smaller than normal. Large meals cause distension and discomfort. Try eventually to decrease the number of meals, or re-adjust to a normal feeding routine.

Exercise: The queen will naturally decide for herself when she requires exercise and when she needs to rest. However, encourage exercise whenever possible, since a fat queen loses muscle tone and is much more likely to experience difficulty during the birth than one which is more healthily honed.

Pregnancy care

• Give natural foods and avoid chemical preservatives and additives.
• Avoid the pregnant cat coming into contact with insecticides, detergents, CFCs and sprays of any kind. These can have an adverse effect on developing fetuses, especially in the first three weeks.
• At the first sign of pregnancy, treat the queen and her various nests for fleas because they respond to hormones in the pregnant cat's blood by laying even more eggs than usual. Flea sprays however, can be detrimental to the developing fetus.

• Effective, natural alternatives to chemical flea deterrents are garlic and aromatic herbs such as citrus, rosemary, eucalyptus or lavender.
• Worming the pregnant cat is also a necessary procedure, since worms can present a serious health risk to unborn kittens. In the last three or four weeks, the queen should be wormed once a week to avoid infecting the kittens.
• Onions and garlic included in the diet will discourage both fleas and worms. Garlic is very potent when added fresh and raw. As a worm preventative, give a herbal combination of garlic, southernwood and sage, finely cut or powdered and made into pea-sized pills with flour and honey. Give two every morning before food.

As pregnancy progresses, the abdomen becomes distended and the urge to rest will become increasingly frequent

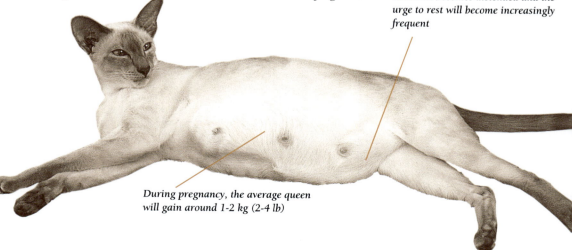

During pregnancy, the average queen will gain around 1-2 kg (2-4 lb)

Preparing for the Birth

Endless wanderings

During the last fortnight of her pregnancy, the queen will wander around the house looking for the perfect place in which to have her babies. Her wanderings will alert you to the fact that her time is near.

Kittening box

Provide your cat with a box in which you would like her to have her kittens, although your heavily pregnant cat may or may not agree with you. Cut a hole in the center of one side of a high-sided, draftproof cardboard box, to enable the queen access to and from the litter tray. The hole is placed centrally so that early learning kittens cannot climb out of the box and hurt themselves. For greater security, place a cardboard box upside down in another similarly sized cardboard box so that you now have a kitty home with an enclosed roof. The doorway should be cut through

Pawnote:

You can only encourage your cat to kitten in your specially prepared box. Do not force her to, otherwise this could cause stress and she might even desert her kittens.

both layers of cardboard. A clean, disposable flannelette sheet placed on top of several sheets of newspaper inside the abode completes this ready-made den.

In the days after the birth, for the purposes of cleaning and/or laying down clean sheets or blankets, you can quickly remove the top box and check the kittens when mum emerges for her food and water and toilet routine. Site this box in a quiet, traffic-free area in your home, but an area which is frequented by yourself, so that the queen recognizes your familiar movements and routine without being stressed by disturbance from others.

Birthing equipment

Most experienced mothers go ahead in a most efficient way and give birth without the assistance of their owner. In fact, the majority of self-respecting mothers will resent this. Strange scents deposited while handling her new-borns will only confuse and alienate her. However, some inexperienced females or those whose birth is not straight-forward may need your help.

Here follows a list of items which could be useful:
- Cotton wool swabs – to mop up mucous from kittens' mouths and noses and for cleaning rear ends or clearing away uneaten placental material
- Blunt-ended scissors – to cut the umbilical cord if mother forgets or cannot do so because she is busy delivering another baby
- Surgical spirit – to sterilize the scissors between use
- Petroleum jelly – to ease the vagina if birth is difficult
- Veterinary disinfectant – to disinfect your hands, etc.
- Clean sheets and news-papers to replace those soiled at the birth

In emergencies

If you are concerned about your queen's condition before or during labor or after the litter has arrived, night or day, call your vet immediately for advice or a visit.

The Birth

First stage: You will know the birth is imminent when your queen refuses her food, is restless and repeatedly visits the kittening box but will not settle down. This stage can be brief or it may last as long as 24 hours. Make a note of the time as this and each following stage occurs. Most queens need no help at all but will be comforted by your presence in the background. If she can be persuaded, give your queen raspberry leaf pills to ease her forthcoming labor and the birth of her kittens.

Second stage: The queen purrs loudly, or sometimes she may be seen breathing heavily or panting. A clear discharge can be seen leaking from the vagina, which the queen will constantly lick away. She can still be restless and walking around the house at this stage. This is the beginning of her labor and can last up to six hours, though this is not usual.

Third stage: There are visible contractions. A bubble and then a head may be seen and following a strong contraction, the head will be born, followed quickly by the rest of the body. The queen will break the sac and vigorously wash the kitten, clearing the nose and mouth and massaging the newborn with her rough tongue.

Fourth stage: Placental matter will be expelled from the vagina. Mother will chew through the umbilical cord and will generally, unless another kitten is on its way, eat the placenta, or she may eat it later. Intervals between each kitten born can vary from 10 to 60 minutes. Make notes of the time of each birth and any particular circumstances accompanying the birth.

Immediate aftercare

When all the kittens have been born, the proud mother will settle down to give them their first feed. Offer her a bowl of warm milk with egg yolk and glucose to replenish energies at this time.

When it is all over, clean up the nest, handling the kittens as little as possible. If necessary, place a warm hot water bottle well under a clean blanket with a fresh flannelette sheet on top. Keep the room at a comfortable ambient temperature of at least 21°C (70°F) for several days.

Birthing Problems

When to help

Complications may occur with the birth, and not all queens are good mothers. However, do not interfere unless the queen is obviously distressed.

Some kittens will be larger than others and may get stuck part way out of the vulva. If this occurs, wash your hands and lubricate the vulva with a little petroleum jelly. Grasp the kitten firmly and carefully ease it out as the mother bears down.

As each kitten is born – and an average litter comprises five or six – very carefully and with the minimum of handling remove newly born, cleaned-up kits to a safe corner of the kittening box. If these are in danger of becoming chilled, move them back to the mother who may try to nurse them between births.

Keep track of every amniotic sac or placenta. Sometimes the sac ruptures and the kitten is born without one, it having been left behind. It will most probably precede the birth of the next kitten. If one remains and has not appeared after 24 hours, seek veterinary help immediately. To delay is SERIOUS and could mean infection of the uterus or peritonitis.

Should the queen ignore a newly born kitten, you will need to clear its nose and mouth of the membrane to enable it to breathe. When it is breathing satisfactorily, remove the sac completely and rub the kitten dry with the cotton wool swabs or a clean towel. Sterilize blunt-ended scissors and with a piece of cotton, tie this round the umbilical cord about 2.5 cm (1 in) from the navel. Cut the cord on the side of the placenta. DO NOT ever pull on the cord since this will damage the kitten. Under normal circumstances, the queen will bite or chew through the umbilical cord, but since you are doing it on this occasion, you need now to encourage the kitten to suckle.

Call the vet

- If there is uterine inertia – the queen takes a long time to give birth, she is placid, sleepy and movements of the uterus and frequency of these is sluggish.

- Violent though progressive labor which does not produce a kitten and the queen becomes exhausted

- Breech birth – if a kitten's head or limb(s) are trapped within the birth passage

- Blockage in the birth passage – sometimes a dead kitten will block the birth passage

- Miscarriage – accident, infection, stress or fetal abnormality are some of the reasons for a miscarriage

---

Caesarean births

Sometimes the vet may consider delivering the queen's kittens by Caesarean section. This is performed when abnormal birthing conditions exist and is primarily carried out with the aim of saving the life of the queen. A Caesarean delivery often complicates future normal deliveries. If the same complications repeat themselves, the owner may well be advised to consider spaying the queen.

Problems with kittens

Open-eyed kittens: Normal kittens are born with their eyes closed and these can be expected to open at around the eighth day. Premature kittens are sometimes born with open eyes. While some of these kittens can be reared satisfactorily, the majority fade out very quickly.

Cleft palates: Often a genetic fault and common in blue-eyed white cats, kittens tend not to survive due to their being unable to suck their mother's milk. Those less severe cases that do survive can sometimes undergo surgery to repair this defect.

Deformed kittens: Some kittens are born with easily identifiable deformities, e.g. misshapen limbs, etc. Some may have internal deformities such as "flat chests" or misplaced organs. If any of these render the kitten unable to live a full and normal life, euthanasia should be considered.

Post-Natal Care

Caring for the queen

Pamper your queen with small amounts of her favorite foods and comforting drinks of warm milk and honey.

Nutritious food

During the first four weeks of a kitten's life, progressively higher nutritional demands are made upon the mother cat. Depending on age, size and nature of the cat, she may need to be fed more frequently than twice a day. If necessary, during these all-important four weeks, your queen may ask to be fed on demand. Go along with this, for the time being, but ensure her meals are light yet nutritious.

Vitamin supplements?

Well-balanced proprietary canned cat foods interposed with fresh, home-cooked meals should supply all the vitamins, minerals, calcium, proteins, cereals and carbohydrates that the nursing queen will need. Unless she is obviously undernourished, there should be no necessity for extra vitamins and supplements, with the exception of the occasional vitaminised cat treat snack. An excess of some additives can cause serious health hazards, so if in doubt consult your vet.

Check it out

Your queen has presumably delivered all placental material successfully.

If not, seek veterinary advice immediately. After around 24 hours, check that vulval discharge is now only small amounts of clear fluid. Bleeding indicates internal hemorrhage which could be life-threatening.

Signs and symptoms of problems

These conditions could be fatal. Consult your vet immediately.
Metritis: Brown, smelly vulval discharge indicates infection
Mastitis: Swollen and inflamed teats
Pyometra: Accumulation of fluid in the uterus, loss of appetite, high fever and vulval discharge

Haemorrhage: Indicates internal bleeding

Weak kittens

Fading kitten syndrome: One kitten in a litter may be born underweight, fail to suckle or is deformed. These are often ignored by the cat and owners can try to hand-rear these kittens, but they usually die.
Bad-doers: In the same class as the above kittens, but there is an element of hope for these, which are "off-color" and fail to suckle well. With commitment and dedicated hand-feeding, the owner may succeed in rearing a "bad-doer." If they do survive, they are not usually very healthy in adulthood.

Early Kitten Care 1

Fostering

If the queen's milk is insufficient to support her litter, has dried up altogether or the cat herself has died, providing the kitten(s) have had a reasonable start on mother's milk, you can take on the task of bottle-feeding the kitten yourself. Alternatively, use a foster mother. This would be a lactating queen (pedigree or non-pedigree) whose litter has died or has only one or two kittens to feed and is able to accept more. If you are a breeder, you may already have a lactating queen with kittens in your household. This would be the ideal solution to keeping your milk-less kitten(s) alive and well. Also, as feline mothers are notably wary of alien scents, particularly of kittens still bearing the smell of their own mother, to come from the same household would be a bonus for the abandoned kitten(s). Lactating bitches have also been known to take on the young of other animal species, so if your pet dog has recently had pups, you could be in luck.

Bottle-feeding

To take on the nurturing of a tiny kitten means a 24-hour round-the-clock lifestyle for the first week, gradually tapering off until the kitten is weaned. Using a dropper or specialized kitten feeding bottle, kittens should be fed every two hours for the first week. Thereafter, the frequency of the feeds should be decreased and the amount increased.

Kittens at two weeks old should be fed every four hours. Ask your vet for details of special formula kitten milk.

Week one

At one week old, the kitten is around 15 cm (6 in) long. Apart from brief forays to her feed and water bowls and trips to the litter tray, the queen will spend all her time feeding, cleaning, licking under small tails to stimulate bowel and bladder movements and keeping her babies warm. The kittens are unable to maintain body heat for themselves and rely on mother's warm tummy. They are able to crawl towards their mother if she has accidentally pushed one away.

Week two

At two weeks, the kitten is growing rapidly with a body length of around 17.5 cm (7 in). Now, with her internal organs returning to normal, mother cat spends a little more time away from her kittens. The kittens "knead" or tread their mother's abdomen with their forelegs to

stimulate milk flow. They can also be heard purring while feeding. They can extend their soft claws, eyes begin to open and vision matures rapidly.

Week three

At about 20 cm (8 in) long, the kittens' hearing and eyesight develop further. They can now find their way around the nest by sight rather than by smell. They can also recognize their mother by sight, rather than by her warmth and smell. Some co-ordination of the legs enables them to take their first steps. Milk teeth start to break through the gums. Mother may leave her kits for up to an hour at a time. Still dependent upon her for nourishment, they begin to initiate their own feeding times.

Early Kitten Care 2

Week four

At about 21 cm (8½ in) long, the kittens are beginning to wander around. The queen may at this point move the kittens to another nest-site. The kitten now regulates its own body temperature, balance improves and in addition to recognising her by sight, it can also hear its mother's voice. They now make hissing sounds and fluff up their coats in threatening situations. This stage is important and could have a bearing on the kitten's future behavior.

Weaning

The more adventurous kittens in the litter may now be ready to eat small amounts of solid food. Weaning is a gradual process and started only when the mother's milk is obviously not satisfying the kittens. This can be as early as three weeks or as late as six weeks. Start with milky foods, specially formulated weaning foods or human baby foods.

When a kitten begins to show an interest in its mother's food bowl is the time to introduce a little poached white fish, mashed in milk, gradually introducing finely chopped or minced chicken, mashed vegetables in meat gravy and, of course, the specially formulated canned kitten foods. The proprietary brands contain all the vitamins and supplements a growing kitten will need – including the calcium and phosphorus needed for rapidly growing bodies. Home-cooked food may need additional supplementation and you should consult your vet about this.

Plenty of clean, fresh water should always be available but canned milk diluted with water is a good alternative. Feed diluted milk and water with egg yolk and glucose beaten in as a nutritious extra.

Week five onwards

Your kittens will be around 22.5 cm (9 in) to small cat size at 5-12 weeks old. Solid foods become more important and under the watchful eye of mother, eating and subsequent litter training become main activities with play becoming increasingly evident and important. They will imitate their mother's responses and activities and will become ever more aware of relationships and their immediate world.

At around 7-8 weeks, play-fighting and toys assume importance, and feline responses and behaviors are progressively evident. Often non-pedigree kittens are now introduced to their new homes, but it is not advised that pedigrees should leave the breeder until 12-14 weeks of age. The necessary first vaccinations can be given prior to this period. But since maternal antibodies received via mother's milk would prevent the kitten from making its own, final doses of vaccine should be left as late as possible before leaving the breeder.

Preventing Pregnancy

Neutering males

All cats not required for breeding purposes should be neutered and males can be castrated at any age after the testicles have descended. This can be as early as three months old.

Changes

Neutering in itself does not mean an overweight cat, but the will to roam will be curtailed, thus less exercise plus the usual food intake may encourage subsequent weight gain. So, surprise your now loving, home-centered neutered male with a cat aerobics center – and do not forget the importance of play to keep his body and mind alert.

Mechanics of neutering

Castration is a routine operation involving the removal of the cat's testes under general anesthetic. Stitches are not usually required and the cat can be back to normal in a day or two. A male cat can remain fertile up to

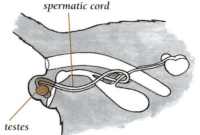

Below: An entire male – the tinted area indicates the spermatic cord and testes which are removed in castration

spermatic cord

testes

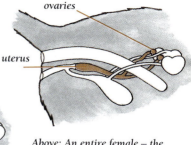

ovaries

uterus

Above: An entire female – the tinted area indicates the ovaries and uterus which are removed in spaying

one month after castration. A newly castrated male cat can give off scents which may arouse or cause aggression in other cats in the household.

Spaying females

Unless a female cat is going to be part of a breeding programme, spaying her is in the best interests of both cat and owner. An entire queen at large can be responsible for hundreds of kittens to be brought into the world with a very uncertain future ahead of them. To prevent this, it is generally advised to spay (neuter) non-pedigree females at 6-8 months of age – earlier if necessary.

Changes

After spaying, a female cat will be much more placid, affectionate and a far more amiable companion, and for you, the problems of managing a cat in oestrus will be non-existent. As for weight gain, the same principles apply to the spayed female

as to the neutered male.

Mechanics of spaying

Spaying or neutering a female cat is a major operation carried out under general anesthetic to remove the ovaries and uterus via an opening in the flank. Spaying should not take place during a female's estrus. A small patch of fur is shaved away from the site of the wound before the operation. This will soon grow back in, albeit slightly darker in color than the overall coat color. As the new hair grows in, the natural color should gradually return.

Use of drugs

As a method of birth control, the use of hormonal drugs will delay estrus. This is a short-term option and will suppress the signs of estrus or postpone a heat period. When the drugs are stopped, estrus should return. Consult your vet on this method of birth control for your queen.

CHAPTER 6

First Aid

Following accidents and emergencies, whether potentially serious or not, your aim will be to keep your cat alive and comfortable until the vet arrives. With a comprehensive first-aid kit in your home, you can probably deal with minor problems yourself. But in all cases, immediate and effective action when your cat needs it most will prevent many a situation from becoming a fatal tragedy.

Being prepared for an emergency will mean that whatever scrapes your cat gets in to, you can rest assured that should he or she come to grief, they will be in capable hands.

This chapter shows you how to cope if your cat is involved in an accident, is injured or suddenly develops a health problem. First aid is an interim measure which could mean life or death for your furry friend. As you know, due to their inquisitive nature and territorial lifestyle, cats are no strangers to injuries or accidents, and at these times it is essential that you administer prompt and effective first-aid action prior to your vet taking over.

Why not familiarize yourself with the following chapter and teach yourself the basics of first aid? At some time in your cat's life, you – and your cat – may be glad that you did!

Preparing for an Emergency

Emergency services

In the case of major accident, contact your vet immediately. Telephone first rather than rush straight to the surgery, then follow the vet's advice regarding immediate first-aid treatment. In minor cases, such as an injured paw or a torn ear, take your cat along to the vet's surgery. If your cat has been involved in a road traffic accident, for instance, and is in shock or is unconscious, call the vet immediately for an emergency home visit.

Day or night

If you are faced with a night-time emergency, assess the state of your cat so that you can explain matters in a sensible manner, then phone your veterinary surgery number immediately. You should get an answerphone message advising you of an emergency service.

If in doubt, get advice

If unsure as to whether your cat requires immediate veterinary attention, **do not hesitate** to phone your vet's surgery to ask for advice. If it is an emergency, the vet or a veterinary nurse will talk through with you any procedures you will need to follow to make your cat as comfortable as possible until help arrives.

When to act

Your cat will need emergency treatment when:
• There is hemorrhaging

First-aid Kit

Every responsible cat person will have a first-aid kit, ready for those emergencies or even minor problems that can often afflict our cats. Turn to Chapter 4 page 75 for the ideal first-aid kit. Keep it stocked up and readily available at all times.

• The cat is unconscious
• The cat is choking, having fits or convulsions
• The cat is in severe pain

When not to panic – yet

You can often administer remedial treatment to minor conditions which may not yet merit an early visit to the veterinary surgery, such as:
• A small local wound, i.e. a thorn in the paw
• Minor wounds due to fighting
• A skin or eye infection
• Foreign body in eye, ear or nose

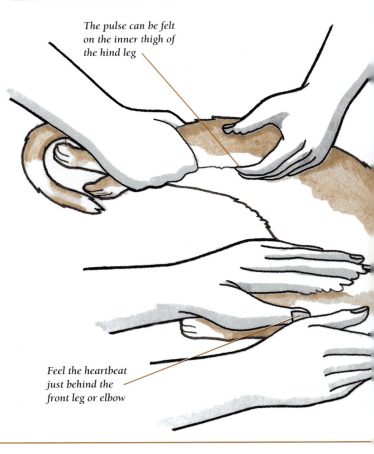

The pulse can be felt on the inner thigh of the hind leg

Feel the heartbeat just behind the front leg or elbow

Checking Life Signs

You have an emergency on your hands if your cat is barely conscious or is totally unconscious. Check and monitor the following essential-to-life functions:

Check breathing

Count the number of breaths either in or out (not both) over a two-minute period. Breaths are on average between 24 and 42 per minute. Note whether breathing is:
a) normal b) labored c) rapid d) shallow e) non-existent.

If breathing is b), c) or d):
• Remove the cat's collar, if any
• Open the mouth
• Pull the tongue forward
• Check the throat for foreign bodies or swelling

If a foreign body is present, grasp the cat firmly, open the mouth and push down the lower jaw. Locate the object and attempt to remove it with the tweezers from your kit. If the above is unsuccessful, contact the vet immediately.

Check for heartbeat

Place the cat on its side, if not already, due to its state. Check for a heartbeat by placing your fingertips firmly on the lower part of the chest just behind the front leg or elbow. If the heartbeat is absent, give artificial respiration immediately – see page 119. If there are signs of life after this is done, call the vet immediately.

Check pulse

The pulse can be felt on the inside of the cat's thigh. Count the beats per minute. In the average cat, these should be around 110-140 beats per minute. An increase or decrease in either breath or pulse rates can be significant.

Check reflexes

Eyelid reflex: Lightly touch the inner corner of the cat's eyelid (closest to nose), taking care not to touch the eyeball itself.
Ear reflex: Gently touch or flick the tip of the ear flap. A cat's ears are very sensitive and if touched they will normally respond by twitching them.
Foot reflex: Gently press or pinch the skin between the cat's toes. If there is any degree of consciousness, the cat would respond by flexing or jerking the leg.

Do's and don'ts:

• **Do** place the cat on its side with head tilted downwards if it is unconscious and/or is suffering breathing difficulties

Pawnote:
Do not persist longer than necessary when checking reflexes – a cat in shock may feel but might be unable to respond to these tests.

• **Do** open the mouth so that the airway is clear
• **Don't** give an unconscious cat medicine, food or liquid by mouth
• **Don't** allow an unconscious cat to lie on one side for more than 5-10 minutes

Shock

Shock is caused by an abrupt fall in blood pressure. A cat in shock will be cold to the touch and the pulse will be weak and rapid. There will be shallow breathing at an increased rate and extremities will be very cold. Place the cat in a warm, quiet, darkened room and make it as comfortable as possible. Keep the cat warm by wrapping it loosely in the silver foil or bubble wrap from your first-aid kit. The hot water bottle, half filled with medium hot water and wrapped in a blanket to protect the cat, will also help maintain body heat. Ensure that the cat's breathing is not restricted.

Accidents

If your cat is involved in an accident, whether in the house or out of doors, contact your vet as soon as possible. If, for instance, haemorrhaging is taking place and urgent attention is required, ask a friend to telephone your vet to say that you are on the way. Only delay this if you think resuscitation techniques or other life-saving steps should be taken before the journey.

Moving an injured cat

To move your injured or unconscious cat with as little trauma to the animal as possible, you will need a blanket or a large, strong towel. Lay this out flat and gently lift the cat onto it. Get help from another person and each of you grasp two corners of the "stretcher." If the cat is unconscious, ensure that its airway is clear (see page 119). If conscious, you may need the assistance of the other person to steady the patient.

Handling an aggressive injured cat

Often after an accident, a cat may resent being handled and become suspicious and aggressive – even towards its owner. Talk reassuringly to the cat and then quietly place a blanket or towel completely over its back (see page 48). Making sure that the legs are tucked inside the blanket, securely restrain all movement by firmly wrapping the blanket around the cat. Leave the head exposed. Maintain a firm grip on the wrapped cat until he is safely placed in his carrier and the lid is closed.

WARNING

• If there is the opportunity before you tend to an unco-operative cat following an accident, don a pair of gloves to protect your hands.
• If fractured or broken limbs are suspected, very carefully lift your cat onto a blanket. Avoid moving its body unnecessarily, keeping the injured limb uppermost.
• Do not attempt to diagnose your cat's condition for yourself. He or she will need a complete check-up by a trained vet before treatment begins.
• When a cat is in pain, injured or even during kittening, it will often purr loudly and continuously. Do not take this as a signal that all is well.

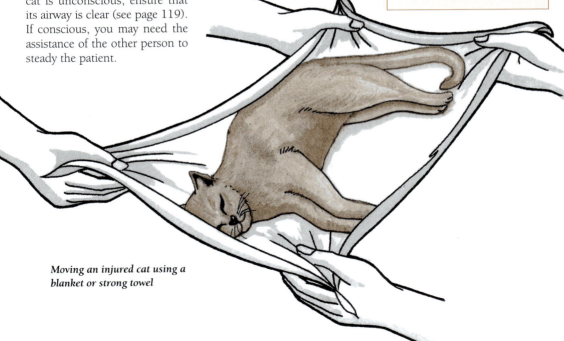

Moving an injured cat using a blanket or strong towel

Resuscitation

Artificial respiration

Respiratory failure and heart failure can happen, for instance, because of drowning, electric shock or poisoning. If your cat has suffered heart failure and has stopped breathing, the heart must be restarted again within a few minutes in order for him to survive.

1. Lay the cat on its side and check that the airway is clear. Open the mouth and look down the back of the throat.

2. Remove obstructions, if any, and pull the tongue forwards. This should stimulate breathing and cause the cat to regain consciousness.

3. If your cat still remains unconscious, place both your hands on the chest and gently apply pressure. This will expel air from the lungs and allow fresh air to fill them. This should be repeated every five seconds – bearing in mind that if the cat does not regain consciousness within two or three minutes, other methods should swiftly be implemented.

Cardiac massage

If there is still no sign of a heartbeat or breathing, place the two fingers of each hand flat on either side of the cat's chest, just behind the elbows. Apply intermittent pressure in a "cough-like" manner at a rate of two per second. After every four compressions, give your cat artificial respiration (see above) for two breaths. Keep checking for a heart or pulse beat (as shown on page 117) and carry on compressing the chest until you feel a pulse beat or until your vet arrives.

Mouth-to-mouth resuscitation

Mouth-to-mouth or mouth-to-nose resuscitation will enable air to fill the lungs. An alternative option is to breathe simultaneously into the cat's nose and open mouth.

1. Encircle the cat's head with one hand and extend the neck by lifting up the chin with the mouth in a closed position.

2. Take a breath and then breathe a little air into your cat's nostrils. The cat's rib cage (chest) should rise.

3. Pause for a two-second rest and then repeat. Repeat this at about 30 breaths per minute.

If spontaneous breathing does not resume after five or six minutes, if the gums and tongue are blue, there is no heartbeat, the pupils of the eyes are dilated and there is no sign of movement of the eyes, the cat is no longer alive.

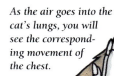

As the air goes into the cat's lungs, you will see the corresponding movement of the chest.

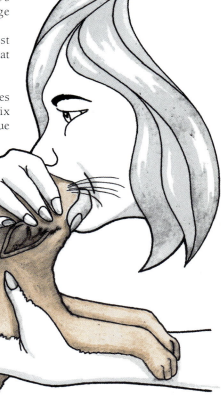

Choking/Foreign Bodies

The signs of choking include:
• Retching and convulsive choking noises
• An inability to close the mouth properly
• Saliva dribbling from mouth
• The cat claws at the side of its mouth with the front paws. This indicates that a foreign body is stuck in the throat, across the roof of the mouth or between the teeth.

1. Quickly make the decision to either take your cat to your vet or try to deal with the problem immediately yourself, and get a friend to call the vet.

2. If the cat is on the verge of collapse and gasping for air, open its mouth and with the aid of your small torch, try to identify the object.

3. Use the tweezers to loosen and remove the offending item. If unsuccessful, turn the cat upside down to try to dislodge the object.

Removing other foreign bodies

Eyes: Grit and grass seeds are the most common objects to become lodged in a cat's eye. Do not allow your cat to paw at it. Carefully hold open the eyelid and examine the eye. If the object has penetrated the eyeball, do not remove it. Contact your vet immediately. If the object is loose, apply 1-3 drops of olive oil to the eye to float it out. If unsuccessful, contact your vet for immediate advice or take your cat to the surgery.

> **WARNING**
> • If, having moved the object, your cat's tongue has turned blue, take hold of it by the scruff of the neck in one hand and the two hindlegs in the other and swing the cat vigorously backwards and forwards to clear the airways.
> • If you are alone at the time of choking, **do not** leave your cat to go and call the vet. His or her best chances are now in your hands.
> • However, a dangerous object such as a fish hook caught in the cat's throat should be left for your vet to deal with. Meanwhile, facilitate your cat's breathing as best you can.

If possible, enlist the help of someone else while you attempt to remove or dislodge the obstruction.

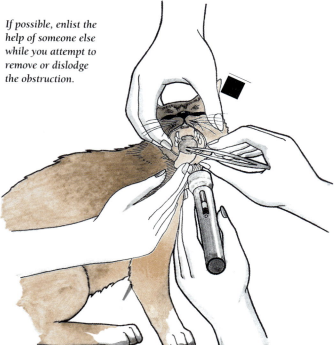

Nose: Do not attempt to remove the object. Apply a cold compress to soothe irritation and/or control bleeding, if any. Contact your vet for immediate advice or take your cat to the surgery.

Ears: Gently examine the ear. If a foreign body is visible, apply 1-3 drops of olive oil to float it out. If this is unsuccessful, contact your vet immediately. Do not make repeated attempts to remove the object.

Paws: Seeds and burrs, etc. can become embedded between the toes, and splinters, thorns and glass can get stuck in a cat's paw pads. If you can, remove the object by hand or tweezers. The cat will continually worry at the spot and may remove it himself.

Drowning/Poisoning

1. If you are able to rescue your cat, quickly dry him off with a towel and immediately turn him upside down to help drain the water from his lungs. Or, pick him up firmly by the back legs and whirl him round to allow centrifugal force to drive out the water. Ask someone to get veterinary assistance quickly.

2. Meanwhile, get your cat into a warm room and lie him on a towel. Check for heart beat and breathing. If both appear to be absent, give cardiac massage and artificial respiration, checking for heartbeat and pulse as shown on page 117, until the vet arrives. It is essential to keep the cat warm.

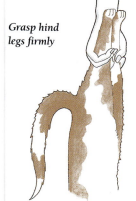

Grasp hind legs firmly

Warning

For all cases of poisoning, contact your vet as soon as possible – these are first-aid measures only. Where there are no specific first-aid instructions, do nothing except make your cat as comfortable as possible and await your vet's arrival.

Signs of poisoning

Signs that your cat has been in contact with, or eaten, a toxic substance can be:

- Vomiting
- Diarrhea
- Convulsions
- Nervous reactions/behavior
- Salivation
- Burns to mouth and/or skin
- Paralysis or coma
- Hemorrhage

Do's and don'ts

Do call your vet immediately you suspect that your cat has been poisoned, and if you know the type or name of the poison involved, telephone the details to your vet.

Do keep the container or package of the poison likely to have affected your cat and give it to your vet.

Don't try to make the cat vomit.
Don't delay. Take your cat to the veterinary surgery straight away.

Removing paint or tar from the coat

Your cat's first reaction will be to lick the coat. Try to prevent him doing this. Soften the contaminated coat immediately with the petroleum jelly from your first-aid kit. If there are patches of heavily contaminated fur, cut these away very carefully with scissors. Using a cat or baby shampoo diluted with warm water, wash away as much of the contaminant as possible. Dry your cat with a towel and wrap him in another one to keep him warm and to prevent him from licking his coat.

Common poisons – emergency first-aid

Types	Signs	First aid
Rodent poison (containing arsenic)	Paralysis	De-contaminate coat
Rodent poison (containing warfarin)	Stiffness, diarrhea, hemorrhaging	Await vet
Horticultural sprays	Vomiting, diarrhea	De-contaminate coat
Paints	Nervous signs, paralysis	Await vet
Tar	Burnt mouth	De-contaminate coat
Wood preservatives	Vomiting, convulsions, coma	Demulcent – a soothing agent, such as milk
Aspirin	Vomiting, liver damage	Demulcent
Insecticides	Nervous signs, salivation, convulsions	De-contaminate coat; await vet

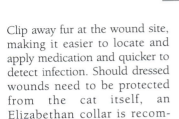

Treating Wounds

Clip away fur at the wound site, making it easier to locate and apply medication and quicker to detect infection. Should dressed wounds need to be protected from the cat itself, an Elizabethan collar is recommended (see page 101).

Warning: Never bandage a limb too tightly, since this could constrict blood flow.

Minor cuts and scratches

Deal with these at home using equipment from the first-aid kit. Care should be taken to keep wounds clean to ensure that they do not become infected.
• **A non-urgent** appointment with the vet is required unless stitches are necessary and/or the wound becomes infected.

Bites

Clean the wound thoroughly and apply veterinary antiseptic and sterile dressing. Calendula (lotion or ointment) can be applied directly to the wound to promote healing. Bandage accordingly. Keen attention should be paid twice daily to the wounds until healed, since bites can become infected very quickly.
• **A same-day** appointment with the vet is recommended. Antibiotics may be given in the first instance and certainly if signs of infection become evident.

Puncture wounds

These are potentially very dangerous both because of severe damage to the body and bacterial contamination. Sterilise the wound and apply an appropriate dressing (as for dressing bite wounds). Cover a punctured or pierced eyeball with sterile dressing and keep in place with a bandage (see page 123).
• **Immediate** veterinary attention is required. According to the location and severity of the wound, antibiotics will be given.

Further treatment will be as recommended by the vet.

Deep lacerations

Staunch the blood flow (see below), apply sterile dressing and bandage. If bleeding is present but does not involve arterial damage (this will mean severe blood loss), Arnica ointment applied to the wound site will help to stop the bleeding. Give single drops of Bach Flower's Rescue Remedy by mouth for shock following injury. Keep the cat warm with blankets or a hot water bottle.
• **Urgent** veterinary attention is required. Hospitalization, anesthetic and stitches/sutures may also be involved. Antibiotics may be prescribed. Further treatment and/or visits to the vet will be required.

Severe wounds

See accidents and moving an injured cat, page 118. Contact your veterinary surgery immedi-

Staunching the blood flow

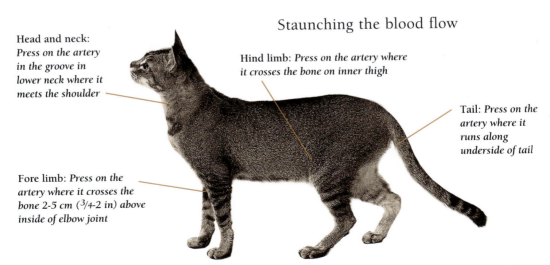

Head and neck: *Press on the artery in the groove in lower neck where it meets the shoulder*

Hind limb: *Press on the artery where it crosses the bone on inner thigh*

Tail: *Press on the artery where it runs along underside of tail*

Fore limb: *Press on the artery where it crosses the bone 2-5 cm (3/4-2 in) above inside of elbow joint*

Bandaging Wounds

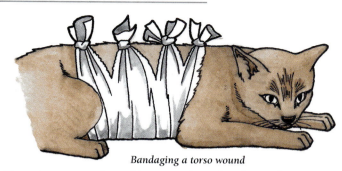

Bandaging a torso wound

ately. See below for how to stop the bleeding. Offer single drops of Bach Flower's Rescue Remedy by mouth for shock following injury. Do this only if your cat is fully conscious. Keep the cat warm with blankets or a hot water bottle.

• **Urgent** veterinary attention is required. Notify the vet so he or she will be ready to receive your cat at the surgery. Following assessment and check-up, appropriate treatment will be administered, including x-ray and subsequent diagnosis, followed by possible surgery and/or hospitalization.

Stop the bleeding

If your cat has been injured and is bleeding heavily, contact your vet for advice **immediately**, then staunch the flow of blood with a gauze dressing. Bleeding should gradually cease and stop after around two minutes. If not, apply another dressing over the top of the first one. Secure with a cotton bandage to keep all in place. Maintain pressure on the relevant pressure points.

Bandaging an eye wound

For minor wounds and/or to stop bleeding, apply a gauze pad. Then clean with veterinary antiseptic and cover with sterile dressing. Place a fresh gauze pad over this and then bandage. Keep the degree of wrapping of the bandage even throughout.

Open wounds

Always cover an open wound with sterile gauze or gauze impregnated with lanolin.

Minor wounds: For instance to the leg. Cover with the dressed gauze – this should fit securely around the leg with a slight overlap. Secure with adhesive tape.

Paw pad wounds: Clean the wound site and place small pieces of cotton wool between the toes to prevent rubbing. Wrap the foot in appropriately sized sterile gauze, again with a slight overlap and an overhang at the toe end. Secure this with adhesive tape. Close together the overhang with adhesive tape. Bring the tape from under the foot and over the toes. Secure all with tape placed around the paw.

Bandaging an eye wound

Place the gauze pad over the affected eye and secure with the elastic bandage, taking it round the head and fixing with adhesive tape as shown.

Torso wounds

With extensive injuries, burns or bruising, a "body bandage" will be required to prevent further injury on the way to the vet's or to give protective cover to one or more dressed wounds in that area. Cut the two opposite sides of a rectangular piece of clean sheeting to make tails, place the cat in the middle of the rectangle and tie the strips together over its back, as shown in the illustration above.

When using the cotton or the wide elastic (crepe) bandage, make a two-thirds overlap at every turn.

Bites and Stings

Bee and wasp stings

Most cats – and kittens – are attracted to flying insects and often, if the insects are bees and wasps, the result can be a painful sting with sometimes a serious outcome. The paws and mouth of the cat are the most vulnerable places.

Bee sting: Bathe with a weak solution of sodium bicarbonate (bicarbonate of soda). Dilution: One teaspoonful per cup of water.

Wasp sting: Bathe with vinegar. Dilution: 50:50 with water.

In both cases, an ice pack can be used to reduce swelling. If the sting is visible, it will appear to be a splinter in a red, swollen area, and you may be able to remove it with tweezers (see illustration below). Urgent veterinary attention is required if the cat becomes disorientated, unsteady or has breathing problems.

Snake and spider bites

In most instances of snake bite, you will not have seen it happen and so will be unable to identify the type of snake involved. If you did see the incident, try to visualise a description of the snake, because this will help with the treatment. The cat will appear stunned and will stare with unblinking eyes. There will be little movement of the limbs.

Snake bite: Fang incisions will be seen as two puncture marks. Slow down the venom by applying a cold compress and a pressure bandage just above the bite.

Place the cat in its carrier and keep it quiet to slow down blood flow from the site of the bite. Urgent veterinary attention is required.

Spider bite: If possible, try to identify the spider. If it remains at the site of the attack, capture it in a sealable jar and take this with you to the veterinary surgery so that appropriate treatment can be given. No immediate signs on the cat's body may be evident. If you suspect spider bite and your cat is agitated, hissing or appears to be in a state of shock, seek urgent veterinary attention.

Toad venom

Some toads secrete venom on their skin, and if the cat picks up the toad in his mouth, it will become painful and inflamed. If possible, flush out the cat's mouth and avoid inhalation of any poisonous fluid. Wipe the mouth and keep him quiet. Urgent veterinary is required.

Cat bites

These may not be immediately evident. If the cat is an unneutered wanderer, the owner should be aware that fighting is part of their cat's lifestyle, so regular checks are advised. See page 59 for injuries sustained during cat fights. Urgent veterinary attention is required. If infection and an abscess is present, the site may need to be lanced and drained by a vet. Antibiotics will be given to control bacterial infection and eliminate recurrence of the abscess.

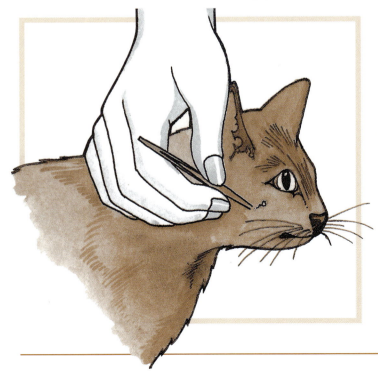

Burns

Scalds

A heat burn or scald can be cooled down by immersing the cat in cold running water. This should be continued for around 10 minutes. Meanwhile, get someone to contact the vet. If immersion in cold water is not possible, wrap your cat in a clean sheet or towel to exclude the air. Shock is associated with burns (see page 117 for Shock). **Urgent** veterinary treatment is required.

Electrical burns

Usually associated with chewing through cables and wires, the tongue and inside mouth will suffer burns. Switch off the current before touching the cat, or use a brush or other wooden utensil to remove the live wire. If heart failure has occurred, see page 119 for how to resuscitate. **Urgent** veterinary attention is required.

Sunburn

Cats with white or pale colored coats are extremely susceptible to sunburn. Owners of these cats should ensure that they are not exposed to hot, direct sunlight. If this is impractical, sunblock (SPF 20 plus) should be applied to nose, ear tips and other parts where the skin is vulnerable. See page 77 and 86 for sun-burn treatment and care. **Immediate** veterinary attention is required when sunburn has taken place. Ensure that all thinly furred parts are protected by sunblock.

Heatstroke

Your cat will be restless, distressed and will pant. Give him a cold running water bath, cover him with cold soaked towels and continue to dowse him in cold water for 10 minutes. **Immediate** veterinary attention is required.

Hypothermia and frostbite

Hypothermia: This means an abnormally low body temperature, usually induced by cold temperature conditions or extreme shock. This is a life-threatening condition and warmth is essential. Wrap the cat in foil or bubble-wrap and utilise the hot water bottle. See page 117 under "Shock" for maintaining body heat. **Urgent** veterinary attention is required.

Frostbite: Caused by exposure for long periods to severe cold (see page 77). Parts such as paws, ear tips and tails become numb and may be completely frozen. Immerse the affected part(s) in warm water to restore circulation. Early treatment is essential to avoid the onset of gangrene or the decay of tissue due to interrupted blood supply. **Urgent** veterinary attention is required.

Ensure sun-block is applied to to nose, ear tips and other parts where the skin is vulnerable.

My Cat's Care Record

Purrsonal details:

Pedigree name:...
Pet name:..
Breed & breed no /type:...
Birthday:...................................... Sex:......................................
Name of dam:............................... Name of sire:..........................
Coat color:................................... Eye color:...............................
Distinguishing marks, if any:...

Veterinarian's name & address:

....
....
....
....
Tel no:..
Emergency no:...

Date of 1st vaccination:...............................
Due date of annual booster:.........................
Other vaccinations:....................................
....
....
....
....

Medical record:...
Illness:...
Dates visited vet:.......................................
Medication:...
Illness:...
Dates visited vet:.......................................
Medication:...
Neutered/Spayed:......................................
Date of operation:......................................
....

Feeding likes & dislikes:...............................
....

Breeder's name & address

....
....
....
....
Tel no:..
....

Stud owner:...
Tel no:..
Date of first litter...
Names/Sex of kittens:..................................
....
....
....

Boarding cattery:.....................................
Name & address:..
....
....
Tel no:..
Useful addresses:....................................
....
....

Useful Addresses

**For a pet behavioural counsel-
lor in your area contact**
Association of Pet Behaviour
Counsellors
PO Box 46
Worcester WR8 9YS

US cat organizations
The International Cat Association
(TICA)
PO Box 2684
Harlingen TX 78551

Cat Fanciers' Association (CFA)
PO Box 1005
Manasquan NJ 08736-0805

Canadian cat organisations
Canadian Cat Association (CCA)
220 Advance B1 Ste 101
Bramptom, Ontario L6T 4J5

Australian cat organisations
Royal Agricultural Society Cat
Control of NSW (RAS)
GPO Box 4317
Sydney NSW 2001

Feline Control Council of Victoria
Royal Showgrounds
Epsom Road
Ascot Vale VIC 3032

Index